# New Challenges

Michael Harris
David Mower
Anna Sikorzyńska
Lindsay White

Students' Book **3**

# Contents

| Unit/Page | Language | Skills |
|---|---|---|
| **Get Ready** | | |
| A Back to School (pp. 4–5) | **Grammar:** Questions | **Study Help:** Classroom language |
| B My World (p. 6) | **Grammar:** Indefinite pronouns | **Study Help:** Vocabulary |
| C What's New? (p. 7) | **Key Words:** Places at Home and School **Grammar:** Present Perfect | **Study Help:** Grammar and mistakes |
| **1 Schools** | | |
| **Get Ready** (pp. 8–9) | **Key Words:** School Facilities | **Listening:** The *Challenges* characters  **Reading:** An advert  **Speaking:** Schools |
| 1 Home Schooling (pp. 10–11) | **Grammar:** Present Simple and Present Continuous | **Reading:** Interview with a family |
| 2 Boarding Schools (pp. 12–13) | **Sentence Builder:** Comparison *(not) as* + adj + *as*; *(not) the same as*; *more … than* **Word Builder:** Multi-part verbs | **Reading:** UWC education  **Reading Help:** Scanning for information  **Speaking:** Schools and rules |
| 3 Arriving (pp. 14–15) | **Key Expressions:** Preferences  **Sentence Builder:** Verbs of preference + *to/-ing* | **Reading and Listening:** The *Challenges* story  **Speaking:** Talking about preferences  **Everyday Listening:** An announcement  **Listen closely:** Weak forms of *a, are, of, have* |
| Across Cultures 1 (pp. 16–17) | **Word Builder:** Dependent prepositions | **Reading:** Schools in the UK  **Speaking:** School, study and exams; game  **Project:** Your ideal school |
| **Study Corner 1** (p. 18) | | **Study Help:** Using your coursebook |
| **2 Talent** | | |
| **Get Ready** (p. 19) | **Key Words:** Abilities | **Listening:** Young celebrities  **Reading and Speaking:** Questionnaire; talking about personal talents |
| 4 Magicians (pp. 20–21) | **Grammar:** Past Simple and Past Continuous | **Reading:** Magicians |
| 5 Hidden Talent (pp. 22–23) | **Word Builder:** Verbs with prepositions **Sentence Builder:** Linking with *when* and *while* | **Reading:** Hidden talent  **Speaking:** Famous women |
| 6 Auditions (pp. 24–25) | **Key Expressions:** Opinions – agreeing/disagreeing | **Listening:** Musical extracts  **Reading and Listening:** The *Challenges* story  **Speaking:** Celebrities  **Everyday Listening:** Interview for a holiday job  **Pronunciation:** Sounds /t/, /d/, /θ/ and /ð/ |
| Your Challenge (p. 26) | **Text Builder:** Organisation; linking with *too, also, as well* and *either* | **Writing:** An email  **Writing Help:** Getting ideas for emails, letters and postcards |
| **Understanding Grammar** (p. 27) | Question tags | |
| **Study Corner 2** (p. 28) | | **Study Help:** Similar words |
| **3 Health** | | |
| **Get Ready** (p. 29) | **Key Words:** Health (1) | **Listening:** Lifestyle changes  **Speaking:** Lifestyle questionnaire |
| 7 Disease (pp. 30–31) | **Key Words:** Diseases  **Grammar:** The passive | **Reading:** Disease |
| 8 Home Remedies (pp. 32–33) | **Word Builder:** Prefixes for opposites, e.g. *antibacterial, unpleasant*  **Sentence Builder:** *important to do, good to do* | **Reading:** Home remedies  **Reading Help:** Skimming  **Speaking:** Health advice |
| 9 Under the Weather (pp. 34–35) | **Key Words:** Health (2)  **Sentence Builder:** *(not) good enough to*; *too busy to*  **Key Expressions:** At the Doctor's | **Reading and Listening:** The *Challenges* story  **Speaking Help:** Preparation for roleplays  **Speaking:** Doctor and patient roleplay  **Everyday Listening:** At the doctor's  **Listen closely:** Main stress |
| Across Cultures 2 (pp. 36–37) | **Key Words:** Food; Nutrition  **Word Builder:** Word families, e.g. *barbecued, steamed, fried* | **Reading:** A health time bomb  **Speaking:** Health quiz  **Project:** A survey |
| **Study Corner 3** (p. 38) | | **Study Help:** Storing words/expressions |
| **4 People** | | |
| **Get Ready** (p. 39) | **Key Words:** Personality Adjectives | **Listening:** Teenagers describing themselves  **Speaking:** Personality questionnaire |
| 10 Problem Page (pp. 40–41) | **Key Words:** Feelings  **Grammar:** Speculating | **Reading:** Problem page letters |
| 11 Generation Gap (pp. 42–43) | **Word Builder:** *make* and *do* **Sentence Builder:** *let/make someone do something* | **Reading:** Family arguments  **Speaking:** Roleplay |
| 12 In Town (pp. 44–45) | **Key Expressions:** Phone Calls  **Listen closely:** *it isn't* and *it's not* | **Reading and Listening:** The *Challenges* story  **Speaking:** Roleplays  **Everyday Listening:** Phone calls  **Listening Help:** Specific information |
| Your Challenge (p. 46) | **Text Builder:** Reference words; adverbs, e.g. *actually, luckily* | **Writing:** Emails  **Writing Help:** Checking |
| **Understanding Grammar** (p. 47) | Personal pronouns | |
| **Study Corner 4** (p. 48) | | **Study Help:** Memorising vocabulary |

| Unit/Page | Language | Skills |
|---|---|---|
| **5 On the Move** | | |
| Get Ready (p. 49) | **Key Words:** Transport | **Listening:** People talking about their hobbies<br>**Speaking:** Travel, transport and danger |
| 13 TV Traveller (pp. 50–51) | **Key Words:** Jobs  **Grammar:** Present Perfect | **Reading:** A TV presenter |
| 14 On Safari (pp. 52–53) | **Key Words:** Animals (1)  **Word Builder:** Compounds<br>**Sentence Builder:** -ing words | **Reading:** Holiday adverts  **Speaking:** Questionnaire |
| 15 The Boat Trip (pp. 54–55) | **Key Expressions:** Making Suggestions | **Reading and Listening:** The *Challenges* story<br>**Speaking:** Problem solving  **Everyday Listening:** Travel agent<br>**Pronunciation:** Sounds /g/, /dʒ/ and /ŋ/ |
| Across Cultures 3 (pp. 56–57) | **Word Builder:** Confusing words | **Reading:** Nomads  **Speaking:** Moving house<br>**Project:** Touring your country |
| Study Corner 5 (p. 58) | | **Study Help:** Explaining words |
| **6 Films and Books** | | |
| Get Ready (p. 59) | **Key Words:** Films and Books | **Listening:** Describing films and books<br>**Speaking:** Books and films; game |
| 16 Bond, James Bond (pp. 60–61) | **Key Words:** Films  **Grammar:** Predictions | **Reading:** Bond films |
| 17 Classics (pp. 62–63) | **Key Words:** Books and Reading<br>**Word Builder:** Multi-part verbs<br>**Sentence Builder:** *although* and *however* | **Reading:** Classic books  **Reading Help:** Difficult words and phrases<br>**Speaking:** Film and book quiz |
| 18 The Long Goodbye (pp. 64–65) | **Sentence Builder:** *I don't know when/where/how/who/what to …*<br>**Key Expressions:** Instructions and Reasons | **Reading and Listening:** The *Challenges* story<br>**Speaking:** Game<br>**Listen closely:** Weak forms |
| Your Challenge (p. 66) | **Text Builder:** Paragraphs; linking words | **Writing:** Film review |
| Understanding Grammar (p. 67) | Present Perfect and Past Simple | |
| Study Corner 6 (p. 68) | | **Study Help:** Multi-part verbs |
| **7 Music** | | |
| Get Ready (p. 69) | **Key Words:** Music | **Listening:** Musical extracts; musical tastes  **Speaking:** Music survey |
| 19 Sixty Years of Pop (pp. 70–71) | **Grammar:** Defining relative clauses | **Reading:** The history of pop |
| 20 Music Makers (pp. 72–73) | **Key Words:** Instruments<br>**Word Builder:** Adjective suffixes, e.g. *musical, useful, interesting*  **Sentence Builder:** Linking with *either … or, neither … nor, both … and, not only … but also* | **Reading:** Unusual musical instruments<br>**Speaking:** How musical are you? |
| 21 The Song (pp. 74–75) | **Key Expressions:** A Short Presentation | **Reading and Listening:** The *Challenges* story<br>**Speaking Help:** Short presentations  **Speaking:** A presentation<br>**Everyday Listening:** Battle of the bands<br>**Listen closely:** Identifying individual words |
| Across Cultures 4 (pp. 76–77) | **Word Builder:** People and places, e.g. *Jamaican, Jamaica* | **Listening:** Musical extracts  **Reading:** Caribbean music<br>**Project:** A biography |
| Study Corner 7 (p. 78) | | **Study Help:** English through songs |
| **8 Discoveries** | | |
| Get Ready (p. 79) | **Key Words:** Science | **Listening:** Street survey  **Speaking:** Ranking discoveries |
| 22 Great Inventions (pp. 80–81) | **Grammar:** Unreal conditionals | **Reading:** Famous inventions and discoveries |
| 23 Land of Giants (pp. 82–83) | **Key Words:** Animals (2)  **Word Builder:** Noun suffixes *-ry, -tion, -ance, -ence, -ist*<br>**Sentence Builder:** *much, a lot, even, a bit* | **Reading:** A time the world forgot<br>**Reading Help:** Identifying the main point<br>**Speaking:** Information gap; game |
| 24 A Surprise (pp. 84–85) | **Key Expressions:** Offers and Requests | **Reading and Listening:** The *Challenges* story  **Speaking:** Roleplays<br>**Everyday Listening:** TV programme  **Listen closely:** Contractions |
| Your Challenge (p. 86) | **Text Builder:** Linking with *so, so that, to, because*; reference words | **Writing:** Emails |
| Understanding Grammar (p. 87) | *a lot of/lots of, much/many, a little/little, a few/few* | |
| Study Corner 8 (p. 88) | | **Study Help:** Self-assessment |

Student A Activities (p. 89)
Student B Activities (p. 90)
Time Out! (pp. 93–105)
Word Bank (pp. 106–111)
Questionnaire scores and answers (pp. 91–92)
Fact or Fiction answers, Irregular verb list (p. 92)

## A Back to School

Get Ready

### Warm-up

**1** Write two good things and two bad things that happened during your holiday. Then tell the class.

*Good things: We went to the mountains. I learnt to dive.*
*Bad things: I broke a tooth. I lost my phone.*

### Grammar: Questions

**2** Match the questions (1–7) and answers (a–g). Listen and check.

1  **What** did you do in the holidays?
2  **Where** did you go?
3  **Why** did you go there?
4  **Whose** party did you go to?
5  **How** did you get there?
6  **Who** did you see?
7  **When** did you come home?

a) Ireland – we went to Dublin.
b) My cousin's. He was eighteen last month.
c) Some friends from school.
d) On Sunday evening.
e) We went away for two weeks and the rest of the time I was at home.
f) We went by train.
g) Because we all like Irish music.

4

# Revision

**4** Write questions about the missing information in the sentences.

1  I met **?** in the holidays. Who … ?
*Who did you meet in the holidays?*
2  **?** stayed with her grandparents. Who … ?
3  **?** fell in the lake. What … ?
4  We ate a lot of **?** . What … ?
5  **?** went to a theme park. Who … ?
6  We cooked **?** on the campfire. What … ?
7  He bought a **?** . What … ?

## Your Turn

**5** Write four sentences about your holiday but leave gaps.

*I went to _____ .*
*I met _____ .*

**6** Work in pairs. Ask and answer your questions.

A  *Where did you go?*
B  *I went to the lakes.*

## Reading and Listening

**3** Read and listen to the conversation between two friends. Complete the questions in the table.

A  What did you do in the holidays?
B  I went camping with my whole family: my parents, sister, aunt, uncle and my cousins, Frank and Millie.
A  That sounds great.
B  Yes, it was good fun. We always have lots of competitions: worst singer, untidiest tent, slowest swimmer. I won the prize for untidiest tent!
A  Who did you beat?
B  This year, I beat Frank. He usually wins that competition. Last year, I got the prize for worst karaoke but I didn't win this year.
A  Who beat you?
B  Well, we're all bad singers! In the end, Millie beat me. She sang *I Will Always Love You* and it was terrible.
A  I'm not going to ask your family to join my band.

| Question about the object of the verb. | Who _____ you _____ ? I beat Frank. |
|---|---|
| Question about the subject of the verb. | Who _____ you? Millie beat me. |

## Study Help: Classroom language

- Complete the classroom language questions with the words in the box.

  | mean   repeat   spell   understand |

  1  Can you __*repeat*__ that, please?
  2  How do you _____ 'caravan', please?
  3  I'm sorry, I don't _____ .
  4  What does 'caravan' _____ , please?

- Write down

  a) a new English word from this page.
  b) an English word with difficult spelling.
  c) an English word with difficult pronunciation.

- Work in pairs. Ask and answer questions about the words.

  A  *What does 'karaoke' mean?*
  B  *It's when you sing the words of the song while the recorded music plays.*

5

# B My World

## Reading

**1** Match the captions (1–6) with the cartoons (a–e). There is one extra caption.

1 This party's terrible. I can't speak to anybody.
2 Surprise! Everybody is here!
3 Waiter! There's something swimming in my soup!
4 I'm bored. I've got nothing to do.
5 I know my phone's somewhere in my bag.
6 Hello! Is anybody there?

a

b

c

d

e

## Grammar: Indefinite pronouns

**2** Complete the table with words from the cartoon captions in Exercise 1.

|  | Person | Place | Thing |
|---|---|---|---|
| affirmative 100% | _____ | everywhere | everything |
| affirmative | somebody | _____ | _____ |
| negative | nobody | nowhere | _____ |
| negative sentences and questions | _____ | anywhere | anything |

## Practice

**3** Complete the paragraph with indefinite pronouns.

### My area

I really like where we live. I know ¹*everybody* in our building so it's very friendly and safe – ² _____ ever locks their front door. The only problem is that it's an old building so there is ³ _____ for people's cars. They have to leave them ⁴ _____ on the street.
There are lots of teenagers in the flats so there's always ⁵ _____ to spend time with at the weekends. We usually do ⁶ _____ like watch a DVD or listen to music because there isn't ⁷ _____ to play tennis and football.
There is a small food shop near the flats but they don't sell ⁸ _____ . For example, if you want ⁹ _____ fresh, you have to go to the supermarket. Next to the shop is my favourite café. I love ¹⁰ _____ on the menu but I usually have ¹¹ _____ Italian like a pizza or some pasta.

## Your Turn

**4** Write five sentences about your area using the words in the table. Tell your partner.

*There's nowhere to play football in my area.*

### Study Help: Vocabulary

- Look at these ways of storing vocabulary and add words.

| Music | | |
|---|---|---|
| types | people | instruments |
| pop classical _____ | guitarist drummer _____ | piano guitar _____ |

football — sport — tennis
swimming — sport — _____

- Draw a table for holiday words. Use these headings in the columns: *places, activities, transport*.
- Draw a diagram for school subjects, e.g. *maths, science*.
- Work in pairs. Add words to each other's work.

# C What's New?

**Revision**

## Warm-up

1 Look at the Key Words. Which places are not usually in a school?

**Key Words:** Places at Home and School

basketball court   bedroom   canteen
classroom   corridor   hall   kitchen
living room   playground   staff room

## Reading and Listening

2 Read and listen to the dialogue. Are the sentences true (T) or false (F)?

1 ☐ Tom likes the red paint.
2 ☐ Tom knows who put the page on the website.
3 ☐ Snacks were cheaper last term.
4 ☐ Last term, Ana ate chips all the time.
5 ☐ Nic is surprised about Iris.

*It's the first day of the school year. Some friends are talking in the corridor.*

**Nic** Hi, guys. Has anybody seen the canteen?
**Ana** No, I haven't. Why?
**Nic** They've painted it.
**Tom** Yes, I've seen it. It's a horrible red.
**Ana** Yuk!
**Tom** And they've changed the menu. Somebody's put a page about it on the school website. I read it this morning.
**Ana** What's different?
**Tom** Well, they've taken chips and burgers off the menu.
**Ana** Why have they done that? I always have chips. Have the prices stayed the same?
**Tom** No, they haven't. Snacks are more expensive but they haven't changed the price of fruit and vegetables.
**Ana** That sounds okay. Do you know what else is new this term?
**Nic** No, I don't.
**Ana** Guess who has dyed her hair.
**Nic** Oh, I don't know. Who's dyed her hair?
**Ana** Iris. She looks really different. She's dyed her hair blond and she's got new clothes.
**Nic** Really? Has she become a model?
**Ana** Don't be silly!

## Grammar: Present Perfect

3 Complete the table with *has*, *have* or *haven't*.

| Affirmative | Negative |
|---|---|
| I/You/We/They ¹_____ painted it. | I/You/We/They ³_____ changed the price of fruit. |
| He/She/It ²_____ lost weight. | He/She/It **hasn't** seen the canteen. |

| Yes/No Questions | Short Answers |
|---|---|
| ⁴_____ I/you/we/they stayed the same? | Yes, I/you/we/they **have**. No, I/you/we/they ⁶_____ . |
| ⁵_____ he/she/it become a model? | Yes, he/she/it **has**. No, he/she/it **hasn't**. |

| Wh- questions |
|---|
| Who ⁷_____ dyed her hair? Why ⁸_____ they done that? |

## Practice

4 Match the results (1–5) with the reasons (a–e). Write sentences using the Present Perfect.

*1 – e   They've bought new sports equipment.*

1 The gym is better this year.
2 Her hair's black.
3 The books are in boxes.
4 He's healthier.
5 We've got a new English teacher.

a) he / lose weight
b) Ms Neville / left
c) she / dye it
d) the builders / not finish the new library
e) they / buy new sports equipment

### Study Help: Grammar and mistakes

- Read the advice about learning grammar. Find one example of bad advice.

1 Keep a list of your common grammar mistakes.
2 Don't say or write anything unless the grammar is 100 per cent right.
3 Do practice exercises.
4 Play grammar games in class and with friends.
5 Notice the differences and similarities to the grammar in your own language.

- Correct the grammar mistakes.

1 Has he ate all the cake?
2 She have bought a lot of new clothes.

7

# Module 1

- Talk about your school, likes and dislikes.
- Read about schools around the world.
- Listen to school announcements.
- Write about your ideal school.
- Learn more about the Present Simple and Present Continuous.

Jasmin

Matt

# Schools

## Get Ready

**1** Listen to the people in the photos. Make notes about:
- where they are from
- what they like
- what they are good at
- what they want to be

**2** Listen again and complete the sentences with *Matt*, *Jasmin*, *Sam* or *Gwen*.

1 _____ goes to a big school.
2 _____ goes to a small private school.
3 _____ has a good dance teacher.
4 _____ has acting classes at school.
5 _____ has dance classes after school.
6 _____ and _____ play the piano.

**3** Look at the Key Words. What facilities has your school got? Has it got any others?

**Key Words:** School Facilities

art room   computer room   dance studio
football/hockey pitch   gymnasium
indoor/outdoor swimming pool
language laboratory   library   music room
recording studio   science laboratory   stage
tennis courts   theatre

**4** Read the advert. Which things would you like to do?

*I'd like to do drama and I'd like to make a film.*

Sam

Gwen

## Summer courses
PETERGATE SCHOOL OF PERFORMING ARTS

Would you like to be a professional musician, singer, dancer or actor? With us, you CAN do it!

**3-WEEK RESIDENTIAL COURSE IN NORWICH** (185 kilometres from London).

- Music: classes for piano, guitar, violin, flute, saxophone
- Singing • Dance • Drama
- Performances: Students perform a piece of music and a song. Groups produce a short film or play.
- Excellent facilities: theatre, dance studio, recording studio

- Accommodation: shared rooms
- Full board (breakfast, lunch and dinner)
- Large gardens • Tennis court
- Gymnasium • Outdoor swimming pool

Dates: courses begin 15th July and 15th August

**5** Work in pairs. Ask and answer the questions and give reasons for your answers.

1. What is your favourite subject at school?

*My favourite subject is chemistry because I've got a great teacher.*

2. What is your favourite activity in your English class?
3. What is your favourite day of the week?
4. What is your favourite place in the school?

**6** **Speak Out** Tell the class *your* opinions.

1. What extra facilities would you like to have at your school?

*I'd like to have a skatepark near the science laboratories.*

2. What extra classes would you like to have?

9

# 1 Home Schooling

## Warm-up

**1** Look at the web page and the photos. How is home schooling different from your school day?

**Home Schooling in Britain**

**What is it?** Home schooling is when parents teach their children. In Britain, about 50,000 students learn at home.

**Who can do it?** Any parent can decide to teach their children at home. You don't have to be a teacher.

**Why do it?** You can match the day to your children's interests, abilities and learning styles. Children learn at their own speed with people they know and love.

## Reading and Listening

 **2** Read and listen to the interview. Check your answers from Exercise 1.

**John** I'm John Watts, a reporter for the *Daily News*. I'm visiting Sally Atkins and her two children. Ned is fifteen, Leah is ten and they learn at home with their mum. Sally, can you tell me about home schooling?

**Sally** Yes, I can. Today is a typical day. Leah is in the garden. She's drawing plants and writing about them. She loves the natural world. Every Friday she goes to a nature club with other kids. They learn about animals and the environment.

**John** Who decides what she does?

**Sally** Here she is – why don't you ask her?

**John** Hi, Leah. Who decides what you do every day?

**Leah** I do. I talk to Mum about the things that I'm interested in and she helps me. It's great! I don't have formal lessons so I'm never bored. Today I'm making a poster about plants for my nature club.

**John** That sounds interesting. What about you, Ned?

**Ned** It's different for me now because I'm studying for three exams: maths, English and science. I chose the subjects and Mum's helping me to study and revise. Today I'm doing some practice exams. Twice a week, I study physics with another home-school kid, Isabelle. Her dad's a scientist and he's teaching us about energy and force at the moment.

**John** So you *have* got some friends.

**Ned** Of course! I meet them in the park every day to play football.

**3** **Speak Out** Do you think home schooling is a good idea? Would you like to study at home with your parents? Why/Why not? Tell the class.

## Grammar: Present Simple and Present Continuous

**4** Read the sentences (1–4) and match them with the names of the tenses: Present Simple and Present Continuous.

a) _____
1 They **learn** at home.
2 She **loves** the natural world.
b) _____
3 She**'s drawing** plants.
4 I**'m studying** for three exams.

10

# Grammar

**5** Find the sentences (1–4) from Exercise 4 in the text. Match them with the uses (a–d) below. Find more examples in the text for each use.

> **We use the Present Simple to talk about:**
> a) a present state or feeling, _____
> b) an activity we do regularly. _____
>
> **We use the Present Continuous to talk about:**
> c) an activity happening right now at the time of speaking, _____
> d) an activity happening for some time around the time of speaking but not necessarily now. _____

## Practice

**6** Match the people (1–6) with the sentences (a–f).

*1 – b*

| | | | |
|---|---|---|---|
| 1 | a person allergic to chocolate | a) | I'm not eating chocolate. |
| 2 | a person on a slimming diet | b) | I don't eat chocolate. |
| 3 | a history teacher on holiday | c) | I only read magazines. |
| 4 | a teenage girl | d) | I'm only reading magazines. |
| 5 | a student before an exam | e) | I study every day. |
| 6 | a hard-working student | f) | I'm studying every day. |

**7** Complete the sentences with the verbs in brackets in the Present Simple or the Present Continuous.

1 Laura is a good student. She ___*likes*___ (like) school a lot.
2 Jill wants to travel across Siberia next year so she _____ (learn) Russian.
3 Chris is very fit. He _____ (swim) a lot and _____ (go) jogging every day.
4 I'm on a diet. I _____ (not eat) sweets this month.

**8** Complete the interview with Ruby with the correct form of the verbs in brackets.

**I** Tell me about a typical day for you.
**R** Every day is different. I ¹*don't start* (not start) at a regular time. At the moment, I ² _____ (learn) about the stars, so I ³ _____ (do) a lot of things at night!
**I** ⁴ _____ your parents _____ (study) the stars with you?
**R** My dad is but Mum isn't. She ⁵ _____ (hate) being outside in the cold for hours.
**I** ⁶ _____ you always _____ (study) with your dad?
**R** No, I don't. I work with the best person for that subject. For example, Mum ⁷ _____ (teach) me French, art and geography. Dad's a scientist so I ⁸ _____ (do) things like biology with him. At the moment, my older sister ⁹ _____ (study) for a physics exam, so Dad ¹⁰ _____ (help) her and a friend, Ned.
**I** Do you get good grades?
**R** I ¹¹ _____ (not know)! I never ¹² _____ (take) tests or exams.
**I** How do you know if you are learning?
**R** I ¹³ _____ (not worry) about that.

**9** Use the notes below to make sentences about Ned and Ruby. Use the Present Simple and Present Continuous.

**Ned:** do a practice exam today, learn at home, never wear a school uniform, not do a past exam paper on the Internet, play football every day, study for three exams at the moment

**Ruby:** look at the sky this week, make notes today, not go to traditional school, not often work on a laptop, play tennis every weekend, study French with her mum

*Ned is doing a practice exam today. He learns at home.*

## Your Turn

**10** Work in pairs. Describe your school. Use the ideas below and the time expressions in the box. Add your own ideas.

> every day   sometimes   never   often
> at the moment   always   this week/month

- get grades • play sport/music • have lessons
- have tests • train for a match • go on trips
- work with other students • watch films
- put on a play

*We have lessons every day but we don't have tests very often. This week our class team is training for a basketball match.*

**11** Read your descriptions to the class. Which is the most interesting?

**TIMEOUT!** ▶ Page 93, Exercise 1

11

# 2 Boarding Schools

## Warm-up

1 Read the text about two British boarding schools, Roedean and Eton. Are there boarding schools in your country? Would you like to go to one? Why/Why not?

## Reading

 2 Read the text about UWC and match the titles (a–e) with the paragraphs (1–5).

a) fees
b) free-time activities
c) houses
d) general information
e) the first school

### ROEDEAN

Opened 1885 in Brighton, near the sea. 400 girls aged eleven to eighteen (about fifteen per cent are day girls). Three houses. Girls share rooms in groups. Fees: approx. £24,000 per year.

### ETON COLLEGE

Opened in 1440 in Windsor, near London. About 1300 boys aged thirteen to eighteen. Twenty-five houses. No dormitories; pupils have their own study-bedrooms. Fees: approx. £26,000 per year.

 UWC

1 UWC is a movement consisting of thirteen schools and colleges and over 120 national committees, which can be found in five continents. German educationalist, Kurt Hahn, had the idea for the international colleges during the 1950s' Cold War. He believed that young people from all over the world, learning and living together, could help to build international understanding and world peace.

2 On 19th September 1962, the first school, UWC Atlantic College, was opened in Wales. UWC Atlantic College is a mixed boarding school and has 350 students aged from sixteen to nineteen years old. It is more diverse than most schools: the students come from as many as eighty different countries. Life at UWC Atlantic College is not as formal as at some boarding schools. Students don't wear a uniform and there are no compulsory sports or competitions between the houses.

3 In addition to academic work, UWC students take part in community service. Every student must take up a voluntary activity for two afternoons or evenings a week. UWC Atlantic College students can choose from a wide range of activities and services. For example, they can help with sea and beach rescue; work on the college farm where they learn to grow food and take care of the environment or organise activities for disabled children.

4 At UWC Atlantic College, the students live in seven houses. Each house has beds for about forty-eight students and, usually, four students from different countries share a room. Houseparents live with the students and take care of them. The rooms are quite simple and the students share bathrooms. Each student house has a living room with a small kitchen and study rooms. Breakfast, lunch and dinner take place in a beautiful twelfth-century dining room.

5 Anyone can apply to a UWC school or college. There are no restrictions on nationality, religion or politics. The fees are about £23,500 a year but the school chooses students for their ability to learn, not their ability to pay. The organisation helps students if they need money.

12

**3** Look at the Reading Help.

**Reading Help: Scanning for information**
- Read the text quickly to get the general idea.
- Read the questions to see what type of information you need (e.g. names, dates, times).
- Find the paragraph with the information and read it carefully.

**4** Copy the table. Scan the texts from Exercises 1 and 2 and complete the table.

|  | Atlantic College | Eton | Roedean |
|---|---|---|---|
| Location |  |  | Brighton |
| Year opened |  | 1440 |  |
| Type of school | mixed boarding school |  |  |
| Age of students |  |  |  |
| Number of students |  |  |  |
| Number of houses |  |  |  |

**5** Read the text in Exercise 2 again. Are the sentences true (T), false (F) or is there no information (NI)?

1. ☐ All the UWC are international.
2. ☐ The first UWC was in Germany.
3. ☐ Atlantic College students must play sports.
4. ☐ All students at UWCs study in English.
5. ☐ The students at Atlantic College eat all their meals in their houses.
6. ☐ Most students at a UWC are from rich families.

**6** Look at the Sentence Builder. Find two more examples in the text.

**Sentence Builder**
Atlantic College is **more diverse than** most schools.
My school is **as expensive as** Roedean.
Roedean is **not as expensive as** Eton.
The fees at his school are **the same as** at Roedean.
The fees at Atlantic College are **not the same as** those at Eton.
Roedean hasn't got **as many pupils as** Eton.

**7** Compare your school with Atlantic College, Eton and Roedean. Use the Sentence Builder and these words to write sentences.
- activities • big • classes • expensive
- famous • international • old • students

*My school has got more students than Atlantic College.*

**8** Look at the Word Builder. Find the verbs in red in the text and read the sentences.

**Word Builder**
take part in (an activity)
take up (a hobby/activity)
take care of (someone/something)
take place

**9** Rewrite the sentences using verbs from the Word Builder.

1 The exams are in the gym.
*The exams take place in the gym.*
2 Why don't you start to learn Italian?
3 Please look after the baby.
4 She always does something in the school play.
5 Can you feed my cat when I'm away, please?
6 I'd like to start judo next term.

**10** **Verb Quiz** Find these *get* expressions in the Word Bank. You've got two minutes!

1 To enter a bus. _____
2 You do this every morning. _____
3 To enter a car. _____
4 To meet people. _____
5 To be friendly with someone. _____

▶ Word Bank, page 106

## Speaking

**11** Work in pairs. Ask and answer the questions.
Which do you think is better:
1 day or boarding schools?
2 boys, girls or mixed schools?
3 school uniform or own clothes?
4 final exams or project work?

**12** 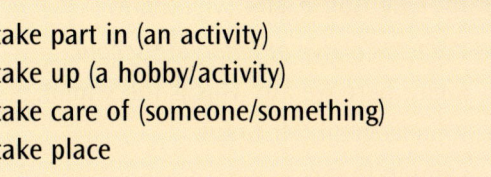 **Speak Out** What rules at your school do you think are unfair? Tell the class.

**Fact or Fiction?**
'Public schools' in Britain are, in fact, expensive private schools
Answer on page 92.

 ▶ Page 93, Exercise 2

# 3 Arriving

## Warm-up

1 Look at the photo. What can you remember about the students?

## Reading and Listening

2 Read and listen to the dialogue. Find the people (and the animal) in the photo.

- Gwen • Jasmin • Matt • Sam • Mr Bywater
- Mr Grant • Benson • Mrs Tyler-Smith

*The four students arrive at Petergate School.*

**Doug** Right, here we are. This is the school.
**Jasmin** It looks great, Mr Grant.
**Doug** Call me Doug.
**Jasmin** Right … er, Doug.
**Doug** That's Mr Bywater over there, one of the music teachers. And that's Mrs Tyler-Smith with her cat, Benson. She's the owner. Come and meet her.
**Mrs T-S** Hello! Did you have a good trip?
**Jasmin** Yes, thanks.
**Mrs T-S** Are you Gwen?
**Jasmin** No, I'm Jasmin. This is Gwen.
**Gwen** Pleased to meet you.
**Mrs T-S** So, you're an actress, Janet.
**Jasmin** Jasmin. Well, I prefer dancing to acting. I really love dancing.
**Mrs T-S** Oh. And you, Helen, sorry, Gwen. You'd like to be a singer. Is that right?
**Gwen** Well, I'd rather be a film director. That's my ambition and I like taking photos.
**Mrs T-S** Really? Well, come in!
**Sam** Hey, it's a big place!
**Matt** I can't stand old houses. I'm allergic to dust.
**Sam** Allergic to dust?
**Matt** Yeah, and cats. I hate going near them. And I don't like dogs much either.
**Sam** Don't you like any animals?
**Matt** I don't mind goldfish. They're okay.
**Sam** Well, there's a cat over there. Look.
**Matt** Oh no! And who's that strange guy with the beard?
**Sam** I think he's one of the teachers.
**Matt** Really? He looks scary.
**Sam** Come on. Let's go in.

**Skills**

**3** Read the dialogue again. Are the sentences true (T) or false (F)?
1 ☐ Doug is friendly to Jasmin.
2 ☐ Mrs Tyler-Smith has a good memory.
3 ☐ Matt doesn't like the place.
4 ☐ Matt is allergic to goldfish.

## Speaking

**4** Complete the Key Expressions from the dialogue with the words in the box.

| hate  like (x2)  love  mind |
| much  prefer  rather  stand |

**Key Expressions: Preferences**

1 I _____ dancing to acting.
2 I really _____ dancing.
3 You'd _____ to be a singer.
4 I'd _____ be a film director.
5 I _____ taking photos.
6 I can't _____ old houses.
7 I _____ going near them.
8 I don't like dogs _____ either.
9 I don't _____ goldfish.

**5** Work in groups. What do people like and dislike about school?

• sport  • rooms (e.g. the library)  • classes
• school lunches  • after-school clubs
• school trips  • exams  • school parties/dances

A *Do you like doing sport at school?*
B *I can't stand sport, I prefer dancing.*
C *I don't mind PE classes and I like swimming.*

**6** 🔊 **Speak Out** Tell the class about your group.

**7** Look at the Sentence Builder. Which sentences are about:
a) general likes/dislikes?
b) something you want to do now or in the future?

**Sentence Builder**

| I **like watching** films. | I'**d like to watch** a film. |
|---|---|
| I **prefer watching** films to plays. | I'**d rather watch** a play. |

**8** Work in pairs. Say true sentences about the ideas below. Use *I like* or *I'd like*.

*I'd like to have acting classes at school.*

• have acting classes  • meet Keira Knightley
• eat Turkish food  • speak English
• go snowboarding  • play the guitar
• visit the UK

**9** Work in pairs. Arrange things to do this weekend, e.g. go to the cinema, rent a DVD, go shopping. Use *I prefer* and *I'd rather*.

A *What would you like to do on Friday night? Would you like to go out or watch TV at home?*
B *I'd rather go out because I prefer going to the cinema to watching TV.*

### Everyday Listening 🔊

🔊 1.12 **1** Listen to Mrs Tyler-Smith and complete the information about summer courses at Petergate.

**PETERGATE SUMMER COURSES**

**Meals**
Breakfast from [1]_____ to [2]_____
Lunch at [3]_____
Dinner at [4]_____
After-lunch concerts at 1.45 on [5]_____ and [6]_____

**Closing times of facilities:**
Rehearsal rooms [7]_____
Theatre/dance studio/gym [8]_____
Swimming pool/tennis court [9]_____
NO NOISE after [10]_____, please!

**Excursions:**
London [11]_____ July
Great Yarmouth (the coast) [12]_____ July

🔊 1.13 **2 Listen closely** Listen to the extracts from Exercise 1. Which of these words can you hear in the sentences: *are* or *a*?

🔊 1.14 **3** Listen to more extracts. Which of these words can you hear: *of* or *have*?

**TIMEOUT!** ▶ Page 93, Exercise 3

# Across Cultures 1

## Warm-up

1 Imagine you are moving to a school in another country. What do you want to know? Write two questions. Then compare your questions with a partner.

*Is there a lot of homework?*

## Reading

2 Read the questions (1–6) at the beginning of the text. Are they the same as your questions?

 3 Read the text about schools in the UK. Match the questions (1–6) with the correct replies (a–e). Two questions are answered in the same reply.

1 – a

### education-info.com

Our family is moving from the United States to London. Keira, (thirteen) and Oliver (fifteen) are worrying about going to school in the UK. (The only one they know about is Hogwarts in the Harry Potter films!)
Can anyone answer our questions?
1 Are schools free in the UK?
2 Are the school subjects the same as in the United States?
3 What's a typical day like?
4 At what age do students start/leave school?
5 Do kids wear a uniform?
6 Do schools have entrance exams?
Thanks for your help!

**Moving Mom**

**a** State education is free so the schools pay for teachers, books, exam fees and any special equipment for science, etc. We (parents) pay for school uniforms and things like rulers, calculators. Also, schools charge for extras like school trips. About ninety per cent of British students go to a state school.
**Jayathome**

**b** I go to a comprehensive school and I study: English, maths 👍, science, technology, history ☹, geography, foreign languages, music, art, sport and citizenship. My school also has after-school clubs for swimming and drama.
**Bestboy@15**

**c** Here, students start primary school when they are five and move to secondary school when they are eleven. At sixteen, students take public exams called General Certificate of Secondary Education. After GCSEs, students can leave school, do a course to prepare for a job or study for A level (Advanced Level) exams (these are necessary for university entrance).
**Retiredheadteacher**

**d** Most schools are comprehensive so they don't have an entrance exam. Secondary schools usually have a uniform. Some schools have simple uniforms with, for example, a shirt, sweatshirt and a dark skirt or trousers. Other schools have more formal uniforms with jackets and ties.
**Dave75**

**e** My school day is 8.40 to 4 o'clock, Monday to Friday. We start with registration. Then we move about the school for different lessons. We have short breaks between lessons and a longer break at lunchtime. Some people eat in the school canteen but I take a packed lunch.
**glittergirl**

**4** Read the text again. Are the sentences true (T), false (F) or is there no information (NI)?

1 ☐ Most British parents pay for their children's education.
2 ☐ British students have to clean their classrooms.
3 ☐ There are after-school activities.
4 ☐ Nobody can leave school before they are sixteen.
5 ☐ Everybody takes A level exams.
6 ☐ A lot of secondary schools don't have a uniform.
7 ☐ Normally there aren't any lessons at the weekend.

**5** Check if your questions in Exercise 1 are answered in the text.

**6** Find compound nouns in the text with these meanings.

1 a school the government pays for
*state school*
2 a secondary school with no entrance exam
3 special clothes students must wear at school
4 the place where students can eat lunch
5 an exam that is the same everywhere
6 the money you pay to take an exam
7 an exam you take to get into a school

**7** Look at the Word Builder. How do you say the phrases in your language?

> **Word Builder**
> study for an exam
> pay for books
> charge for school trips

**8** Complete the questions with words and phrases from Exercises 6 and 7.

1 One person writes about GCSEs and A levels. Which _____ do students take in your country?
2 How do you _____ a test? Do you plan your revision carefully or do it the night before?
3 Do you eat in your _____ ? Why/Why not?
4 Does your school _____ extras like guitar lessons?
5 Who _____ your school equipment like pens, pencils, etc?

## Speaking

**9** Work in pairs. Ask and answer the questions from Exercise 8.

**10 Game** Work in pairs. How much can you remember about British schools? Test your partner. Student A uses the text to ask questions. Students B closes the book and answers.

A *Who pays for the students' books?*
B *Their parents.*
A *No. The school pays for their books.*

### Your ideal school

**1** Think about these things:
- location  • day school or boarding school
- school trips  • boys, girls or mixed school
- number of students in a class  • facilities
- uniform or no uniform  • school rules
- after-school clubs

**2** Plan your description. Make notes on these points:

1 general description (location, type of school, uniform, rules, facilities)
2 a typical school day (classes, lunch, breaks)
3 after school (clubs, activities, trips, homework)

**3** Write your description in three paragraphs.

*My ideal school is near the sea. It's a day school for boys and girls. There isn't a uniform and there aren't any rules. The school has got a music studio, an Olympic-size swimming pool and a computer for every student.*

**4** Work in groups. Read each other's descriptions. Say what you like or dislike about your partners' ideal schools.

# Study Corner 1

## Language Check

### 1 Complete the words in the sentences.
1  We have our chemistry lessons in a l _ _ _ _ _ _ _ _ _ _ _ .
2  Our school has got three tennis c _ _ _ _ _ _ .
3  There is a football p _ _ _ _ _ .
4  I get books from the school l _ _ _ _ _ _ _ .

### 2 Complete the verbs in the sentences.
5  I want to take _____ photography.
6  When I'm ill, my mum takes _____ of me.
7  I'd like to take _____ karate or judo.
8  When my neighbour is away, I take _____ of his dog.
9  He'd like to take _____ in the concert.
10 The school dance takes _____ in the gym.

Vocabulary ☐ / 10

### 3 Put the verbs in brackets in the Present Simple or the Present Continuous.

A  Hi, Alan. What $^{11}$_____ you (do) here?
B  Shh, Fred, don't speak so loudly. I $^{12}$_____ (revise) for my exams. I often $^{13}$_____ (come) to the library. I sometimes $^{14}$_____ (use) the computers here.
A  I $^{15}$_____ (use) my dad's computer at home when my sister isn't on it!
B  Where is she? I want to talk to her.
A  She $^{16}$_____ (play) hockey. They $^{17}$_____ (have) a school competition this week. They always $^{18}$_____ (have) it at this time.
B  Oh yes, I forgot about that. Anyway, why are you here? You hate studying.

A  I $^{19}$_____ (look for) information for the quiz. They $^{20}$_____ (ask) a lot of geography questions and there's a good atlas here.

Grammar ☐ / 10

### 4 Choose the correct word.
A  Would you $^{21}$ love / like to $^{22}$ go / going to the school dance this weekend?
B  Thanks, but I'd $^{23}$ rather / prefer go to the cinema. I love $^{24}$ go / going out with my friends but I prefer $^{25}$ watch / watching films to $^{26}$ dance / dancing. I $^{27}$ can't / don't stand $^{28}$ be / being in noisy places.
A  I $^{29}$ don't / can't mind that – I love $^{30}$ to go / going to clubs and discos!

Communication ☐ / 10

## Feedback

- Listen and check your answers to the Language Check. Write down your scores.
- Look at the table. Check where you made mistakes.

| Wrong answers: | Look again at: |
| --- | --- |
| Numbers 1–4 | Get Ready – Key Words |
| Numbers 5–10 | Unit 2 – Word Builder |
| Numbers 11–20 | Unit 1 – Grammar |
| Numbers 21–30 | Unit 3 – Key Expressions |

- Now do the exercises in Language Check 1 of the Workbook.

## Study Help: Using your coursebook

Find these things in *New Challenges 3*. Which are the most useful for you?

- Key Words • Key Expressions • Word Builder
- Word Bank • Reading/Listening Help
- Sentence Builder • Language Check
- Time Out Magazine

- Match the problems (1–10) with the solutions (a–j).

*1 – b*

**I want to …**

1  find out what's in a module
2  find some tips for reading and listening
3  do some extra reading
4  find answers to word quizzes (e.g. verb quiz)
5  revise vocabulary
6  revise a grammar area
7  do extra grammar practice
8  find useful expressions for speaking
9  do a revision test
10 find some tips for studying

**Look at …**

a) stories in Time Out Magazine
b) the top of the Get Ready page
c) the Workbook Grammar Reference
d) Reading and Listening Help boxes
e) the Workbook or CD-ROM
f) the Word Bank
g) the Language Check
h) Key Word boxes, Word Builder and the Word Bank
i) the Study Help boxes
j) Key Expressions boxes

# Module 2

- Talk about your abilities and express opinions.
- Read about magicians and talented women.
- Listen to an interview and complete a form.
- Write an email to a friend.
- Learn about past tenses and auxiliaries.

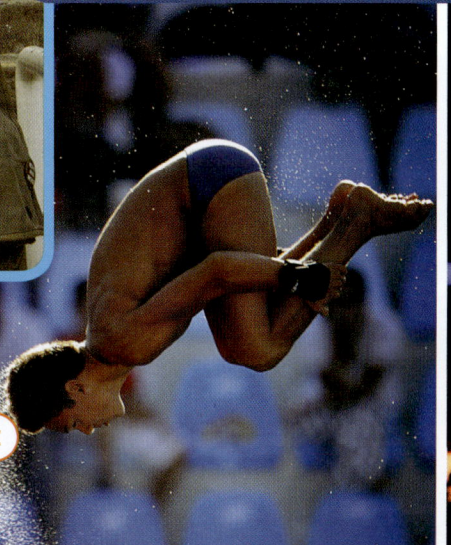

# Talent

## Get Ready

**1** Look at the Key Words. Make guesses about the young stars in the photos (a–d).

*He's a diver. I think he's athletic.*

**Key Words: Abilities**

**Adjectives:** artistic   athletic   creative   imaginative   logical   musical   practical   talented
**Good at/brilliant at:** chess   communicating   gymnastics   languages   making things   maths   music   painting   science   singing   sport   writing

**2** Listen and complete the table.

|  | A famous | From | Born in |
|---|---|---|---|
| **Tom Daley** | diver |  | 1994 |
| **Hou Yifan** |  |  |  |
| **Chloë Moretz** |  |  |  |
| **Justin Bieber** |  | Canada |  |

**3** Who do you think are the most talented film/pop/sports stars in your country and the world?

*I think Matt Damon is the most talented film star in the world.*

**4** Do the questionnaire.

## YOUR TALENTS

**Which of these sentences are true about you?**

1. I like talking in class discussions.
2. I can read maps well and I have a good sense of direction.
3. I can remember songs very well.
4. I am good at sports.
5. I like maths and science.
6. I like making things with my hands.
7. I like reading and playing word games.
8. I am good at doing logic puzzles.
9. I am good at matching colours.
10. I am a good singer.

**5** Find out about your talents on page 91.

**6** Work in pairs. Ask and answer questions about your partner's talents.

A *Are you good at singing?*
B *No, I'm not very musical.*

19

# 4 Magicians

## Warm-up

**1** 🔊 **Speak Out** Have you ever seen a magic show? Tell the class.

*There was a magician at my friend's birthday party. She did lots of card tricks.*

**2** Do you like magic? Why/Why not?

## Reading

**3** Read the texts (a and b). Answer the questions.
1 Which magician had a more difficult childhood? Why?
2 Are the two magicians' tricks similar or different?

### a) DAVID COPPERFIELD

**David Copperfield** (1956–), the best known illusionist of our times, **could** do amazing card tricks in primary school. He **didn't have to** work like Houdini because his family was quite rich. When he was at school, he learnt some magic tricks to impress people. At sixteen, he started teaching magic at New York University.

In his shows in the 1980s and 1990s, he made the Statue of Liberty disappear, walked through the Great Wall of China and levitated across the Grand Canyon. In one show, he flew above the stage with a lady from the audience in his arms, while thousands of amazed spectators **were watching** him.

### b) THE GREAT HOUDINI

**Harry Houdini** (1874–1926) was the most famous escape artist in the world. He was born in Hungary but his family moved to the USA when he was four.

As a child, **he had** to work to help his family – he sold newspapers, cleaned shoes and performed tricks for money. He was only nine when he gave his first public show.

Houdini's most famous acts were escapes. He **could** open locks and handcuffs without a key. (He learnt to open locks when he **couldn't** get an apple pie from his mother's locked cupboard!) He escaped from boxes, underwater tanks and prisons all over the world. Once he escaped from a straitjacket when he **was hanging** on a rope from a high building. Many people tried to copy him but they **couldn't** do his tricks. One man drowned when he **was trying** to escape from a milk tank.

# Grammar

## Grammar: Past Simple and Past Continuous

**4** Name the tenses <u>underlined</u> in the sentences (1–3). Then match the sentences and tenses (1–3) with the uses (a–c).

| 1 He was only nine when he <u>gave</u> his first public show. (_____) | a) regular activities in the past |
| 2 He <u>escaped</u> from boxes and prisons. (_____) | b) longer background activities in the past |
| 3 One man drowned when he <u>was trying</u> to escape from a milk tank. (_____) | c) single events in the past |

**5** Match the sentences (1–4) with the meanings (a–d).

1 He had to work to help his family.
2 He could swim well.
3 They couldn't do his tricks.
4 He didn't have to work.

a) was necessary
b) wasn't necessary
c) had the ability/was possible
d) didn't have the ability/was impossible

## Practice

**6** Complete the text about two other magicians with the verbs in brackets in the Past Simple or Past Continuous.

David Blaine ¹*was walking* (walk) to his car when a poor man ²_____ (stop) him in the street and ³_____ (ask) for some money. Blaine ⁴_____ (take) a one-dollar note from the man. He ⁵_____ (play) with the banknote when it suddenly ⁶_____ (change) into a 100-dollar note.

Howard Jay ⁷_____ (ask) a young woman from the audience to be his assistant. On stage, she ⁸_____ (hold) an empty hat when a large diamond ring ⁹_____ (appear) in it. Her boyfriend ¹⁰_____ (stand) up and ¹¹_____ (ask) her to marry him. The audience ¹²_____ (watch) them all the time. Fortunately, she said, 'Yes'.

**7** Match the speakers (1–4) with the sentences (a–d).

*1 – b*

1 'I had to study a lot.'
2 'I didn't have to study very much.'
3 'I couldn't study very much.'
4 'I could study a lot.'

a) he/she had a lot of time for learning
b) his/her teachers were very strict
c) he/she was a very clever child and found school very easy
d) his/her family was poor and he/she worked in the afternoons to help

**8** Complete the sentences with *had to*, *could*, *couldn't* or *didn't have to*.

1 I'm very good at card tricks; I ___*could*___ already do them when I was five.
2 I _____ do any tricks after I broke my finger.
3 I _____ give a lot of shows to earn enough money.
4 I had two assistants so I _____ do everything myself.
5 I _____ buy all my equipment because magicians only use their own things.

## Your Turn

**9** Use the ideas below to make sentences about what you *could*, *couldn't*, *had to* and *didn't have to* do when you were in primary school.

• come home before 8 p.m.  • speak English
• tidy your room  • watch TV late  • play basketball
• do the shopping  • go cycling  • use the computer
• wash up  • do homework  • feed your pet
• babysit  • read books

**10** Work in pairs. Read your sentences to your partner. Who had to help most at home? Who could do more fun things?

**11** Make two sentences, one true and one false, about things that happened to you last night. Use the Past Continuous and the Past Simple.

*I was walking home when I found some money in the street.*
*I was watching a match on television when the TV set exploded.*

**12** Work in pairs. Guess which sentence is false.

TIMEOUT! ▶ Page 94, Exercise 4

# 5 Hidden Talent

## Warm-up

**1** Work in pairs. Write the names of three famous scientists, travellers and writers from history.

*travellers: Columbus, Marco Polo, Vasco da Gama*

**2** How many of the people on your list are women?

## Reading

**3** Quickly read the texts about the lives of some famous women. Who:
1 were writers?
2 was a scientist?
3 was a traveller?

**4** Read the texts again. Are the sentences true (T), false (F) or is there no information (NI)?
1 ☐ Lady Mary took her children to Turkey.
2 ☐ In the eighteenth century, most British people weren't inoculated against smallpox.
3 ☐ At school, Rosalind Franklin didn't enjoy science lessons.
4 ☐ Rosalind Franklin was friends with Watson and Crick.
5 ☐ Rosalind Franklin wasn't famous in her lifetime.
6 ☐ The Brontë sisters wrote about their own lives.
7 ☐ The sisters had three brothers.
8 ☐ The sisters' poems made them famous.

**5** Find the verbs in **blue** in the text. Complete the Word Builder with the correct prepositions.

| Word Builder | |
|---|---|
| live | *in* |
| learn | 1 |
| work | 2 |
| die | 3 |
| write | 4 |
| travel | 5 |

① Lady Mary Wortley Montagu, a British woman, lived in Turkey at the beginning of the eighteenth century.

While Lady Mary was living in Turkey, she learnt about how the Turkish people inoculated their children against smallpox. Smallpox was a terrible illness: Lady Mary's brother died of it and her face had smallpox scars. At that time, there was no treatment for it in the UK so a doctor inoculated her children in Turkey. When she returned to the UK, she told everyone about the treatment. British doctors didn't listen to her because she was a woman and the idea was foreign. However, the king inoculated his children.

② Rosalind Franklin became interested in science when she was at school. She wanted to study science so she went to Cambridge University where she got a degree in chemistry.

At the beginning of the 1950s, she was doing research into the structure of DNA. Two men, James Watson and Francis Crick, were working on the same problem. When they realised that her photographs were scientific proof of the structure of the DNA molecule, they used her ideas to complete their research. Their discovery of the structure of DNA was one of the greatest scientific discoveries of the twentieth century. When she died of cancer at the age of thirty-eight, most people didn't know how important her work was.

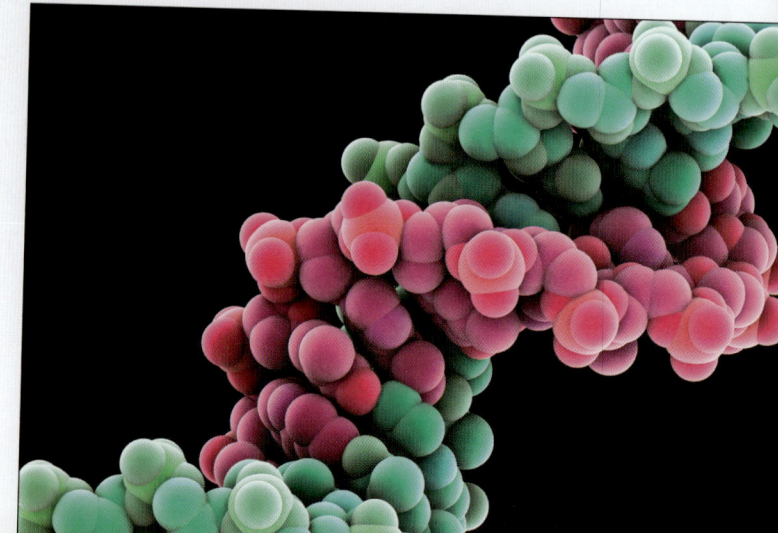

22

**3**

In 1846, three 'brothers', Currer, Ellis and Acton Bell, published their poems. Everyone thought the writers were men but they were three sisters: Charlotte, Emily and Anne Brontë. They used men's names because it was difficult for women to publish books at that time.

When the sisters published their first book of poems, they sold only a few copies. However, in 1847, their novels (Charlotte's *Jane Eyre*, Emily's *Wuthering Heights* and Anne's *Agnes Grey*) made them famous. The young women used their experiences in their books. For example, Charlotte wrote about her terrible experiences at boarding school. People thought the books were shocking and nobody believed that women wrote them. Finally, two of the sisters travelled to London to prove they weren't men.

**6** Complete the sentences with the correct form of the words from Exercise 5.

1 Lady Mary Wortley Montagu _travelled to_ Turkey with her husband.
2 The king _____ inoculation from Lady Mary.
3 The Brontë sisters _____ the north of England with their father and brother.
4 The sisters _____ their experiences in their novels.
5 Rosalind Franklin _____ the structure of DNA.
6 She didn't _____ old age.

**7 Preposition Quiz** Choose the correct preposition in the sentences.

1 I like listening *at / to* music.
2 I sometimes have to wait *for / at* buses.
3 I never worry *on / about* exams.
4 I don't know a lot *about / in* astronomy.
5 I haven't got enough money to pay *by / for* a new computer.
6 I sometimes think *about / in* my old boyfriend.

▶ Word Bank, page 106

# Skills

**8** Look at the Sentence Builder. Which of the underlined words mean:

a) at the same time as?
b) after?

> **Sentence Builder**
>
> <u>When</u> the sisters **published** their first book of poems, they sold only a few copies.
>
> <u>When/While</u> Lady Mary **was living** in Turkey, she learnt about inoculation

**9** Look at the sentences. In which of them can you only use *when*?

1 Lady Mary Wortley Montagu wrote about life in Turkey *when / while* she was living in Istanbul.
2 Lady Mary told people about smallpox inoculation *when / while* she returned to Britain.
3 *When / While* Crick and Watson saw Franklin's photos, they knew they were important.
4 *When / While* Franklin was doing her research, Crick and Watson were doing similar work.
5 The scientists made one of the twentieth century's most important discoveries *when / while* they found the structure of DNA.

## Speaking

**10** Work in pairs. Ask and answer the questions.

1 Which of the women in the texts do you think is the most interesting? Why?
2 What world-famous women do you know from history?
3 What women do you know about from your country's history?
4 What famous contemporary women do you most admire?

**11** 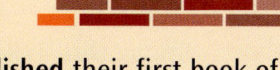 **Speak Out** Why are there still more famous male scientists, composers, artists and leaders nowadays? Which of these reasons do you think are most important? Tell the class.

• women have to look after their families
• it's more difficult for women to be successful
• women are not as interested in fame as men

┌─ **Fact or Fiction?** ─┐
The first woman to win a Nobel Prize was Marie Skłodowska Curie.
◂ Answer on page 92. ▸

**TIMEOUT!** ▶ Page 94, Exercise 5

**23**

# 6 Auditions

## Warm-up

 **1** Listen to Jasmin, Matt, Sam and Gwen's auditions for a concert. How well do you think they played? Give them a score out of five.

**2**  **Speak Out** Tell the class your opinions.

*I think ... played very well. I gave him/her a four.*

## Reading and Listening

 **3** Read and listen to the dialogue. Who:
1. snores?
2. sings in the shower?
3. thinks his performance was very bad?
4. is superstitious?
5. is lucky?

*The group goes to a bowling alley in Norwich after school.*

**Sam** So, what's your room like, Gwen? Our room's quite nice.
**Matt** I don't think so. It's too small and you snore!
**Sam** No, I don't!
**Matt** Yes, you do. I need earplugs!
**Sam** Well, at least I don't sing in the shower like you!
**Gwen** Well, our room is really nice. By the way, what did you think about the audition this morning?
**Sam** I didn't think it was very easy.
**Gwen** Neither did I.
**Matt** It was a disaster! Auditions are horrible.
**Sam** That's true. But honestly, Matt, you were fine.

**Matt** No, I wasn't. I knew before I started because I didn't have my lucky ring.
**Gwen** What?
**Matt** My lucky ring. I sometimes wear it for luck. But I left it in my room.
**Sam** Well, I think superstitions are silly.
**Gwen** So do I. I don't believe in all that stuff.
**Matt** Well, I do.
**Jasmin** Hey, what are you lot talking about?
**Gwen** Matt's 'lucky ring'. Are you superstitious, Jas?
**Jasmin** Well, I never wear yellow on stage. It's unlucky for me. And I've got a lucky bracelet. Look!
**Gwen** Mm, it's really nice.
**Jasmin** Well, it's my turn. Watch. Yes! A strike!
**Sam** I don't believe it!

## Speaking

**4** Look at the Key Expressions.

### Key Expressions: Opinions

| Opinion | Agreeing | Disagreeing |
|---|---|---|
| Our room's quite nice. | That's true. | I don't think so. |
| I didn't think it was very easy. | Neither did I. | I did. |
| I think superstitions are silly. | So do I. | I don't. |
| I don't believe in all that stuff. | Neither do I. | I do. |

**5** Complete the dialogue.
A I ¹_____ the concert was great!
B So ²_____ I! Leona Lewis was brilliant!
A That's ³_____ . But Take That were better.
B I ⁴_____ think so. I think they sang too many old songs.
A I ⁵_____ ! I really enjoyed them. And I think they've got great voices.
B So ⁶_____ I but I prefer their newer songs.

**6** Look at the list of celebrities. Add four more.
• Lionel Messi (footballer) • Kristen Stewart (actor)
• Caroline Wozniacki (tennis player)
• Katy Perry (singer) • Daniel Radcliffe (actor)
• Rafael Nadal (tennis player)
• Dizzee Rascal (singer)

# Skills

**7** Work in pairs. Give your opinions and agree and disagree about the celebrities in Exercise 6. Use these adjectives.
• attractive • brilliant • excellent • good-looking
• great • intelligent • nice • talented

A *Kristen Stewart is attractive but I don't think she's a great actress.*
B *I do. I think she's talented.*

### Everyday Listening

**1** Listen to the interview for a holiday job. Which of the things below can the girl do?

• speak a foreign language • use computer programs • get on with people • repair things • do crosswords • type fast
• use the Internet

**2** Listen again and complete the form.

### YOUR DETAILS
Name: ¹_____ Bayliss
Address: ²_____ , Orchard Rise, Norwich
Date of birth: ³_____ 96
Education: Exams: ⁴_____ , English, history, geography, ⁵_____ and ⁶_____
Work experience: At weekends, works in aunt's ⁷_____ shop
Interests: horse riding, hockey and ⁸_____

**3 Pronunciation** Listen to the four sounds and repeat the words.
1 /t/ hat   3 /θ/ think
2 /d/ had   4 /ð/ then

**4** What sounds are the underlined letters in the sentences?
1 And your date of birth is the fifteenth of the third, ninety-six.
2 I can read and write and understand everything when they don't talk too fast.
3 They're not hard and I can use both of them.
4 Sometimes I work in my aunt's clothes shop at the weekends.

**5** Listen and repeat the sentences.

 Page 94, Exercise 6

25

## Your Challenge

**Writing:** An email

**1** Read Matt's email. Answer the questions.
1. What did Matt do before the course started?
2. What is he worried about?
3. What doesn't he like about Petergate?
4. Which students does he think are talented?

To: finnbutler123@mailme.net
Subject: Norwich                                    attach

Hi Finn,

1 Here I am in the UK! I got here last Sunday. The flight was really long and boring. I stayed with my Uncle Ted in London for four days. I saw the sights and went to a concert as well. Then I got a train up here to Norwich on Friday.

2 Petergate School is okay but the level's a bit too high for me! I played my guitar in the first music class yesterday – I was really bad! And we have to record a song next week! My drama teacher is a weird guy called Bywater. He says he was in TV years ago. Also the director, Mrs Tyler-Smith, has a cat, 'Benson' … and you know I just hate cats!

3 I'm sharing a room with a guy from London called Sam. He's a good singer and plays the piano well, too. There are also a couple of girls. Gwen's from Wales and Jasmin's from Manchester, I think. She's a fantastic dancer – and isn't bad-looking, either.

4 Well, I'm going to bed now. I'm feeling really tired tonight.

See ya!

Matt

### Text Builder

**2** Match the topics (a–d) with the paragraphs (1–4).
a) reason for finishing the email
b) new friends
c) the trip to the UK
d) the school and teachers

**3** Look at the linkers in blue in the text. Which words:
- usually go at the end of a sentence?
- can go at the start or in the middle of a sentence?
- come after a negative verb?

**4** Look at the Writing Help.

> **Writing Help:** Getting ideas for emails, letters and postcards
> - First, think about the situation you are in: Where are you? What are you doing? What is the place like?
> - Think about the letter: Why are you writing? Who are you writing to? What is that person interested in?
> - Think of news: What did you do yesterday/last week? Did you enjoy it? What was it like?

**5** Imagine you are studying at a language school in the UK, United States or Australia. Write an email to an English-speaking friend.

**STEP 1** Use the questions in the Writing Help to think of ideas.

**STEP 2** Write your email. Write about:
- your trip to the UK, United States or Australia
- the school, classes and teachers
- new friends
- a reason to finish the letter

Remember to include linking words.

**STEP 3** Check your email for spelling, grammar and linking words.

**6** Work in groups. Read each other's emails. Which trip sounds the most interesting?

26

# Understanding Grammar: Question tags

**1** Read and listen to the dialogue.

**Zara** Did you watch the match last night?
**Tom** Yes, I did.
**Zara** It was fantastic, wasn't it?
**Tom** Yes – better than the last time they played. That wasn't very good, was it?
**Zara** No, but this time Messi scored a great goal. I think he's brilliant!
**Tom** Do you? I prefer Ronaldo. He's scored more goals this season, hasn't he?
**Zara** That's true. But Messi is the best player in the world at the moment. All the newspapers say that, don't they?
**Tom** But Messi can't run as fast as Ronaldo, can he?
**Zara** Can't he?
**Tom** No, and Ronaldo is older, isn't he?
**Zara** Well, they're both brilliant.

**2** Read the questions (1–2) and match them with Zara's intentions (a–b).

1 Did you watch the match last night?
2 It was fantastic, wasn't it?

a) Zara doesn't know the answer.
b) Zara knows the answer and thinks Tom agrees with her.

**3** Complete the questions with the correct question tags.

| Sentence | Question tag |
|---|---|
| Ronaldo **is** older, | _____ ? |
| All the newspapers **say** that, | _____ ? |
| They **are practising**, | aren't they? |
| He**'s scored** more goals this season, | _____ ? |
| It **was** fantastic, | _____ ? |
| The goalkeeper **played** well, | didn't he? |
| Ronaldo **can run** faster, | can't he? |
| Barcelona **will win** the Champion's League, | won't they? |
| That **wasn't** very good, | _____ ? |
| Messi **can't run** as fast as Ronaldo, | _____ ? |
| Beckham **isn't** in the England team, | is he? |
| Torres **didn't play**, | did he? |
| Chelsea **won't win**, | will they? |

**4** Complete the rules with the correct words.

We use a *positive/negative* tag after a positive statement and a *positive/negative* tag after a negative statement.

## Practice

**5** Complete the sentences with question tags.

1 You can do some card tricks, _can't you_ ?
2 Magicians don't work in the morning, _____ ?
3 Iker Casillas is a very good goalkeeper, _____ ?
4 Footballers earn a lot of money, _____ ?
5 Your parents will come to our matches, _____ ?
6 Spurs have won two matches this year, _____ ?
7 Pelé played in the World Cup when he was seventeen, _____ ?

**6** Work in pairs. Make questions.
➤ Student A, page 89
➤ Student B, page 90

**7** Read the questions in blue in Exercise 1. Does the speaker:
a) agree?  c) show interest/
b) disagree?    surprise?

**8** Respond to the statements with questions to show interest.

1 I'm interested in magic.
   _Are you?_
2 My sister plays for the school team.
3 My dad can't ski.
4 I spent my holidays in Greece.
5 I don't like hot climates.
6 Football is my favourite sport.
7 My mum has just learnt to swim.

**9** Listen to the people. Respond to each sentence. Show interest.

**10** Listen and repeat the responses.

27

# Study Corner 2

## Language Check

**1 Make adjectives from the words in brackets.**

1 She's very _____ and can play the flute beautifully. (music)
2 I'm not a very _____ actor – I always forget my words! (talent)
3 He's very _____ and writes really good ghost stories. (imagination)
4 I'm not a very _____ person. I hate making things with my hands. (practice)
5 My brother's very _____ and is good at all sports. (athletics)

**2 Complete the sentences with the correct prepositions.**

6 Jo is living _____ York at the moment.
7 We learnt _____ the history of theatre in our drama class.
8 The Brontë sisters wrote _____ their experiences in their novels.
9 She's working _____ her school project.
10 My dad often travels _____ the United States for work.

Vocabulary ☐ / 10

**3 Complete the questions.**

11 They're good at tennis, _____ ?
12 He can't play the piano, _____ ?
13 We didn't do very well in the exam, _____ ?
14 You're good at chess, _____ ?
15 Your parents were living in Germany when you were born, _____ ?

**4 Complete the text with the correct form of the verbs in brackets.**

William Shakespeare was born in 1564 in Stratford-upon-Avon. Shakespeare's father was a glove maker and his mother ¹⁶_____ (have) a lot of land. When William was born, his father ¹⁷_____ (do) very well in business but a few years later things ¹⁸_____ (go) wrong. William probably went to Stratford Grammar School and he ¹⁹_____ (can) read and write Latin. When he was eighteen, he ²⁰_____ (marry) Anne Hathaway. William probably ²¹_____ (leave) Stratford to go to London in 1588. Maybe he ²²_____ (have to) leave because of money problems. Anyway, we know that in 1594 he ²³_____ (work) for the most successful theatre company in London. He ²⁴_____ (write) thirty-seven plays and 154 poems. He retired to Stratford in 1611 and ²⁵_____ (live) there until he died at the age of fifty-two.

Grammar ☐ / 15

**5 Complete the gaps with one word.**

A Did you see the game? I thought it was great.
B So ²⁶_____ I. 4–3 with the final goal in the last minute! Games like that are brilliant!
A That's ²⁷_____ . I thought Kakà was the best player.
B Oh, I ²⁸_____ . I thought Ramos was better. And he scored two goals. Kakà was lucky with his goal.
A I ²⁹_____ think so. Anyway, Barcelona played well, too but I didn't think the referee was very good.
B Neither ³⁰_____ I. He made some terrible decisions.

Key Expressions ☐ / 5

## Feedback

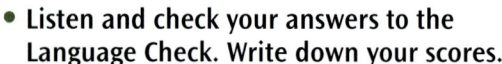

- Listen and check your answers to the Language Check. Write down your scores.
- Look at the table below. Check where you made mistakes.

| Wrong answers: | Look again at: |
| --- | --- |
| Numbers 1–5 | Get Ready – Key Words |
| Numbers 6–10 | Unit 5 – Word Builder |
| Numbers 11–15 | Understanding Grammar |
| Numbers 16–25 | Unit 4 – Grammar |
| Numbers 26–30 | Unit 6 – Key Expressions |

- Now do the exercises in Language Check 2 of the Workbook.

## Study Help: Similar words

Many words in English are similar to words in other languages. You can usually guess the meaning.

- 'International' words, e.g. *taxi*, *hotel*.
- Words from Latin and Greek or a mixture, e.g. television (*telewizor* in Polish, *televisor* in Spanish).
- Be careful with 'false friends' – similar words with a different meaning, e.g. – *a hazard* in English means a danger (*hazard* in Polish means *gambling*).

- Write five words similar in English and your language and two 'false friends'.

# Module 3

a
b
c

- Talk about health; do a roleplay at the doctor's; do a survey.
- Read about disease and home remedies.
- Listen to doctors and patients.
- Write a short report.
- Learn about the passive.

# Health

## Get Ready

**1** Look at the Key Words. Which are a) common health problems, b) treatments?

**Key Words: Health**

acupuncture   an allergy   antibiotics
a cold   flu   a headache   a herbal remedy
insomnia   being overweight   a painkiller
a sports injury   stress   tiredness
a vaccination

**2** Listen to three people. Write B (Brian), Z (Zara) or D (Dan) next to the descriptions (1–9).

1. ☐ played computer games all the time
2. ☐ eats healthy snacks
3. ☐ felt tired all the time
4. ☐ is more relaxed
5. ☐ had a lot of stress
6. ☐ does rowing
7. ☐ lost weight
8. ☐ does yoga
9. ☐ was overweight

**3** Work in pairs. Do the questionnaire with your partner.

### How Healthy is Your Lifestyle?

**1** What kind of drink do you usually have?
a) sweet fizzy drinks
b) tea or coffee
c) fruit juice or water

**2** How many portions of fruit and vegetables do you eat every day?
a) fewer than three
b) three or four
c) five or more

**3** Which of these things do you do?
a) smoke cigarettes
b) spend time in smoky rooms
c) don't go near cigarette smoke

**4** How many times a week do you do physical exercise?
a) never
b) once or twice
c) three times or more

**5** How many hours do you sleep at night?
a) under five hours
b) five to seven hours
c) eight or more hours

**4** Check your answers on page 91. How healthy is your lifestyle?

**5** **Speak Out** How can teenagers in your country get healthier? Tell the class.

*There should be more sports centres and they should be free.*

29

# 7 Disease

## Warm-up

**1** Look at the Key Words. Which of these diseases are common in your country? Which are dangerous?

**Key Words:** Diseases

AIDS   chicken pox   cholera   malaria
measles   mumps   the plague   polio   rabies
smallpox   tuberculosis (TB)   whooping cough

## Reading

**2** Look at the pictures and read the text and the factfile. Choose the best title.

a **NEW DISEASES**

b **FIGHTING DISEASE**

c **AVOIDING INFECTIONS**

**3** In what ways do diseases spread? How can we avoid them? Make two lists.

## Grammar: The passive

**4** Find the sentences in the text and complete them with the correct verb forms.

| Present Simple passive |
|---|
| Nowadays, people [1]_____ against many common diseases. |
| How **is** an infection **passed** on? |
| AIDS **isn't spread** by coughing or kissing. |

| Past Simple passive |
|---|
| Sick people [2]_____ from healthy ones. |
| When **was** penicillin **discovered**? |
| Vaccines **weren't known** until the fifteenth century. |

**5** Find more examples in the text. Complete the rule.

To form the passive, we use the verb _____ + the past participle of the main verb.

---

For thousands of years, there were no epidemic diseases. However, when people started living in towns, infections could spread more easily. When traders and armies travelled from city to city, they brought bacteria and viruses with them and spread infections to new populations. Children were in the greatest danger: in the nineteenth century, fifty per cent of children died before the age of five.

Most infections are spread in the same way: bacteria or viruses are passed on by coughing, sneezing or by touching food with infected hands. People began to understand this as early as the 1300s. During the plague in Milan, the streets were regularly cleaned and the clothes of plague victims were burned.

In the nineteenth century, Ignaz Semmelweiss observed that infection was spread by doctors' dirty hands and recommended washing hands before touching patients. Another early way of avoiding disease was quarantine – sick people were isolated from healthy ones.

Vaccines were first used in the eighteenth century. In 1796, Edward Jenner vaccinated people against smallpox. Nowadays, in many countries, people are vaccinated against many common diseases, such as measles or TB.

### Factfile

Between 1346 and 1350, more than one third of the population of Europe was killed by the bubonic plague (Black Death). When Europeans arrived in America in 1492, they brought their infectious diseases with them. The natives of the Americas were not immune to these diseases. Eight million people died on the island of Hispaniola, where Columbus first landed; the native population of Mexico decreased by ninety-five per cent.

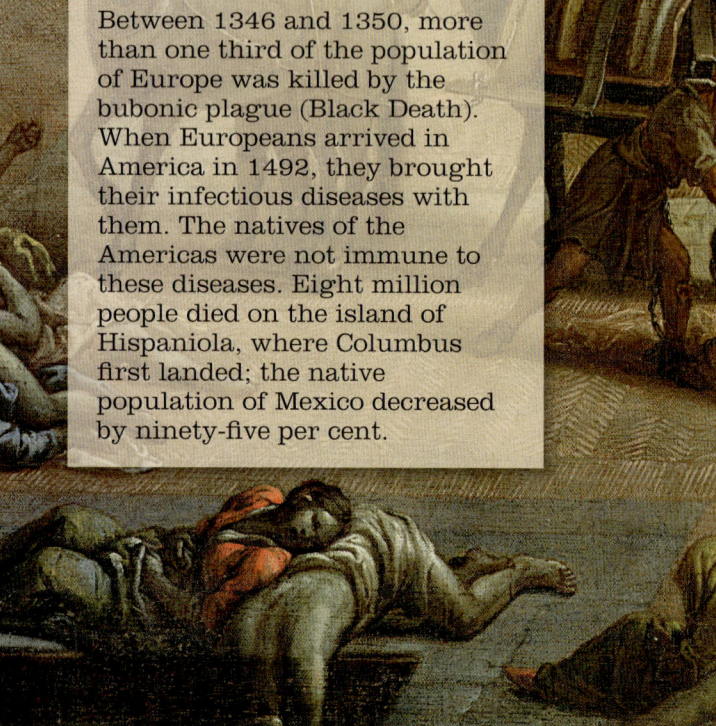

# Grammar

**6** Match the sentences (1–2) with the meanings (a–b).
1. Bacteria kill many people.
2. Bacteria are killed by antibiotics.
a) bacteria are passive (they don't do anything)
b) bacteria are active (they do something)

**7** Read the sentences (1–2) and match them with the uses of the passive (a–b).
1. Infection was spread by doctors' dirty hands.
2. The clothes of plague victims were burned.

> We use the passive:
> a) when we don't know or we don't want/need to say who did something. _____
> b) when we want to stress who or what did something. _____

## Practice

**8** Complete the sentences with the verbs in brackets in the correct form of the Present Simple passive or Past Simple passive.
1. More people ___*are killed*___ by infectious diseases than by anything else. (kill)
2. When _____ antibiotics _____? (discover)
3. About forty million people in the world _____ with HIV which causes AIDS. (infect)
4. Malaria _____ by male mosquitoes. (not transmit)
5. How _____ flu _____ on from person to person? (pass)
6. The plague in Florence _____ by Boccaccio in *The Decameron*. (describe)
7. Many infectious diseases _____ by mice and rats. (spread)
8. AIDS _____ on by sneezing, coughing or touching. (not pass)

**9** Complete the text with the correct forms of the Present Simple passive or Past Simple passive.

> Infections caused by bacteria and viruses ¹ *are treated* (treat) differently. People with bacterial infections ² _____ (give) antibiotics. The first antibiotic, penicillin, ³ _____ (discover) by Alexander Fleming in 1929 but it ⁴ _____ (not use) until the early 1940s. During the Second World War, penicillin ⁵ _____ (produce) on an enormous scale to treat wounded soldiers. Infections caused by viruses ⁶ _____ (not treat) with antibiotics. The patient ⁷ _____ (tell) to drink a lot, stay at home and take painkillers to bring down the temperature. The cure ⁸ _____ (leave) to the patient's own immune system. We can avoid some viral diseases, such as measles or mumps, if we ⁹ _____ (vaccinate). Before we travel to foreign countries, we ¹⁰ _____ (give) vaccinations to protect us from diseases, such as cholera.

## Your Turn

**10** Work in pairs. Make questions in the passive.
▶ Student A, page 89   ▶ Student B, page 90

**TIMEOUT!** ▶ Page 95, Exercise 7

31

# 8 Home Remedies

## Warm-up

1  **Speak Out** How do you treat these health problems in your home? Tell the class.

a) a small cut    b) sunburn    c) a cold

## Reading

2 Look at the Reading Help. Do you 'skim' texts when you read in your own language?

**Reading Help: Skimming**
- The first time you read a text, start by looking through it very quickly to find out what it is about.
- Don't worry about new words or difficult structures. Use the words you know to identify the topic.

3 Use the Reading Help. 'Skim' the text and choose the best title.

a) Kitchen Cures
b) First Aid Equipment
c) Cooked Medicine

4 Work in pairs. Look at these health problems and match them with the home treatments.

| Problems | Treatments |
|---|---|
| 1  a cold | a)  a banana |
| 2  a cut | b)  chicken soup |
| 3  a sore throat | c)  honey |
| 4  a verruca | d)  vinegar |
| 5  a wart | |
| 6  eczema | |
| 7  sunburn | |

5 Read and check your answers from Exercise 4.

It's important to keep a first aid box in your home but a kitchen cupboard also contains lots of simple and inexpensive treatments.

Many people believe chicken soup helps to cure a cold. A doctor in the United States experimented with his grandmother's chicken soup and discovered that it really *is* medicine. The chicken meat contains an amino acid, cysteine, which helps to clear mucus. In addition, the heat of the soup, spices and liquid all help the unpleasant symptoms of a cold. It's good to add some garlic to the soup because it has antiviral and antibacterial ingredients.

Vinegar is a traditional treatment for a cut. It is a disinfectant and it has an ingredient that reduces bleeding. This means that an infection is unlikely to spread. You can also put vinegar on wasp stings and warts. And don't forget, vinegar is great to use for cleaning windows, bathroom taps and kitchen surfaces.

Honey is delicious on toast but 2000 years ago the Romans used it as an antiseptic on their soldiers' wounds. It has an ingredient which stops bacteria growing in an injury. The bacteria can't survive in honey so the wound heals, swelling goes down and healthy new skin grows. Honey also helps sore throats and skin problems like eczema and sunburn.

Bananas are great energy food – and a banana skin can cure a verruca. Verrucas are an uncomfortable foot virus that you can catch anywhere that you walk barefoot. If you're unlucky and you get a verruca, the usual cure is strong chemicals. However, some foot doctors now tell patients to put a piece of banana skin (the white side!) on the foot every night and the results are the same. The soft part of the banana skin contains an antiviral ingredient and this kills the verruca virus.

32

Skills

**6** Read the text again and answer the questions.
1. Why is it a good idea to put garlic in chicken soup?
2. Which ingredient helps to stop bleeding?
3. Why does honey help to cure a cut?
4. What cold symptom can honey help?
5. Where do you catch verrucas?
6. Which part of a banana skin do you put on a verruca?

**7** Look at the adjectives in the Word Builder. Find the opposites in red in the text.

### Word Builder

| Adjective | Opposite |
|---|---|
| bacterial | *antibacterial* |
| viral | 1 _____ |
| pleasant | 2 _____ |
| likely | 3 _____ |
| comfortable | 4 _____ |
| lucky | 5 _____ |
| expensive | 6 _____ |

**8** Complete the sentences with opposites from Exercise 7.
1. That cut looks painful. Put some *antibacterial* cream on it.
2. I'm not going to buy these shoes. They are _____ .
3. Cycling is an _____ way to travel and good exercise.
4. A fish and honey sandwich! That sounds _____ .
5. She's got a cold. She's _____ to go swimming today.

**9** **Adjectives Quiz** Write the opposites of the adjectives in the box. Use *im-*, *in-* or *un-*. Then check your answers in the Word Bank.

| happy | kind | known | fit | necessary |
| polite | tidy | usual | visible |

▶ Word Bank, page 111

**10** Look at the Sentence Builder. Find two more examples of the structure in the text.

### Sentence Builder
It's **important to** keep a first aid box in your home.
It's **good to** add some garlic to the soup.

**11** Use the cues to write sentences. Are they true (T) or false (F)? Check your answers on page 91.
1. ☐ unhealthy / drink a lot of coffee
2. ☐ bad / read in a room without much light
3. ☐ dangerous / cycle without a helmet
4. ☐ good / drink milk before you go to bed

## Speaking

**12** Work in pairs. Write your own health advice (sensible or silly!). Use the ideas below.
• food and drink • sleep • exercise
• eyesight • hearing

*It's unhealthy to have a big meal before you go to bed. (sensible)*

*It's good to listen to loud rap music before breakfast. (silly)*

**13** Work in groups. Take turns to read out your advice. Is it sensible or silly?

**Fact or Fiction?**
Chewing gum takes seven weeks to pass through the human digestive system.
Answer on page 92.

TIMEOUT! ▶ Page 95, Exercise 8

# 9 Under the Weather

## Warm-up

**1** Look at the Key Words. What treatment do you recommend for each symptom? Use the Key Words or your own ideas.

**Key Words: Health**

**Symptoms:** a cough   an earache   a headache   a high temperature   a pain (in your foot/arm/back)   a runny nose   sneezing   a sore throat   a toothache
**Treatment:** drink plenty of fruit juice and water   have an X-ray   stay in bed for a day or two   take cough mixture/medicine/tablets

## Reading and Listening

**2** Look at the photos. How do you think Matt feels? Choose symptoms from the Key Words.

*I think he's got a cough.*

**3** Read and listen to the dialogue and check your guesses from Exercise 2. What treatment does the doctor recommend?

*Matt and Jasmin are working out in the gym.*

**Jasmin** What's the matter, Matt? You look a bit down.
**Matt** I'm fed up. I'm not good enough to be in the dance class.
**Jasmin** You weren't that bad. You shouldn't worry so much. Cheer up! There's a trip to the coast this weekend!
**Matt** Big deal.
**Jasmin** Hey, that's a nasty cough.
**Matt** Yeah, I'm allergic to cats! But seriously, I'm a bit under the weather.
**Jasmin** Well, why don't you go to the doctor?
**Matt** I'm too busy to go.
**Jasmin** Don't be silly. Doug can easily arrange it.
**Matt** Okay, I'll ask him.

*Matt goes to the doctor's that evening.*

**Dr** So, what can I do for you?
**Matt** Well, I've got a bit of a cough. And I've got a sore throat and a terrible headache.
**Dr** Okay, I'll take your temperature … mm, that's quite high. You've got a bad cold. You shouldn't go out for a day or two. And you should drink plenty of water and fruit juice. Here's a prescription for some cough mixture and tablets. You've got to take two tablets three times a day.
**Matt** Okay, thank you.
**Dr** Not at all.

**4** Look at the Sentence Builder.

**Sentence Builder**

| I'm | (not) good enough to be |
| He's | in the dance class. |
| We're | too busy to go. |

**5** Now make similar sentences. Use the cues.

1  I / tired / go out
*I'm too tired to go out.*
2  he / ill / do the exam
3  I / old / drive a car
4  this maths problem / hard / do
5  I / tall / play basketball
6  the bag / heavy / carry
7  he / fit / run a marathon

## Speaking

**6** Look at the Key Expressions. Who says them – the doctor (D) or the patient (P)?

**Key Expressions: At the Doctor's**

What can I do for you? D
I've got a bit of a cough.
I've got a terrible headache.
You've got a cold.
You should drink plenty of water.
You shouldn't go out for a day or two.
You've got to take two tablets three times a day.

**7** Which expression means *have to*?

**8** Look at the Speaking Help.

**Speaking Help: Preparation for roleplays**

- First, think about what to say. Look through Key Expressions and Key Words.
- Write notes (e.g. *have a cold/cough*). Don't write a complete dialogue!
- Practise saying expressions to yourself (e.g. *What can I do for you?*).

**9** Look at the diagram below. Use the Speaking Help to prepare for the roleplay.

**Doctor**

Say hello. Ask what the problem is.
*Hello. What can I do for you?*

**Patient**

Describe how you feel.
*Well, doctor, I've got a sore throat.*

Ask another question.
*Have you got a headache?*

Give more information.
*Yes, I have. And …*

Recommend some treatment.
*Okay. You've got flu. You should take these tablets twice a day. And you've got to drink lots of water.*

Say thank you.
*Thank you very much, doctor.*

**10** Work in pairs. Take turns to be a doctor and a patient. Use the Key Expressions from Exercise 6.

## Everyday Listening

 **1** Listen to two people at the doctor's. Choose the correct answer, a), b) or c).

**Speaker 1**
1  What is the man's problem?
   a) an allergy   b) a cold   c) a headache
2  What is the problem caused by?
   a) cats   b) trees   c) the weather
3  What does the doctor recommend?
   a) exercise   b) fruit juice   c) tablets

**Speaker 2**
4  What has the boy got?
   a) a broken arm   b) a broken leg
   c) a broken rib
5  How did he break it?
   a) cycling   b) playing football   c) running
6  What does the doctor recommend?
   a) running   b) staying in bed   c) an X-ray

**2** **Listen closely** Listen and repeat these expressions. The main stresses are underlined.

1  What's the matter?
2  I'm fed up.
3  You weren't that bad.
4  I'm allergic to cats.
5  I'm a bit under the weather.
6  I've got a bit of a cough.
7  I've got a terrible headache.
8  You've got a temperature.

Page 95, Exercise 9

# Across Cultures 2

## Warm-up

**1** Look at the Key Words. Put them into the categories below. Then add more words to the list.

- fish • fruit • meat • vegetables

**Key Words:** Food

| beans | beef | chicken | garlic | grapefruit |
| lamb | lemon | onion | peach | peas |
| salmon | trout | tuna | | |

**2** What food do you love? What food do you hate?

*I love pizza. I can't stand peas!*

## Reading

**3** Read the list of main food groups (a–e). Put them in order of what you should eat most of (1) to what you should eat least of (5). Look at the picture and check your ideas.

**All the food we eat can be divided into five main food groups:**

a) Fat and sugar
b) Fruit and vegetables
c) Meat, fish, eggs and beans
d) Dairy foods, for example, milk, cheese, yoghurt
e) Starchy foods, for example, rice, pasta, bread for minerals and vitamins and potatoes

**A healthy diet means you eat the right amounts from each group.**

 **4** Read the text about healthy diets. Which diet would you like most/least?

## A health time bomb?

In some parts of the world, it is easy to have an unhealthy diet. Snacks, ready meals and fast food are everywhere but they contain a lot of calories. This is causing health problems like obesity, heart disease, diabetes, strokes and cancer. One North American scientist said, 'If people don't improve their diets, they will die younger than their parents and grandparents. We must learn about healthy eating from other countries.'

The Japanese live longer than other nationalities – and they have the lowest levels of obesity. A typical Japanese meal has a lot of fish and fresh vegetables but they don't eat much meat. Fish like salmon, mackerel and tuna are popular. These contain a fat (omega 3) which is very good for our hearts, brains and eyes. Like most people in Asia, the Japanese get their carbohydrates from rice. Another important part of a Japanese diet is soy beans. These contain a lot of protein and they help to prevent some cancers.

**5** Read the text again. Are the sentences true (T), false (F) or is there no information (NI)?

1. ☐ Seventy-five per cent of people in the developed world have an unhealthy diet.
2. ☐ In some countries, people ate better food in the past.
3. ☐ Lots of people in Japan are overweight.
4. ☐ Japanese people don't eat a lot of meat.
5. ☐ A typical Mediterranean dinner often has fish in it.
6. ☐ Reindeer is a healthy meat.
7. ☐ Cabbage has got more vitamins than other vegetables.

**6** Add new food words from the text to your lists in Exercise 1.

A Mediterranean diet has a lot of fresh fish, fruit and vegetables like peppers, courgettes and aubergines. Bread, pasta or couscous are also an important part of the diet. The fish and vegetables are often barbecued or grilled. Olive oil is used for fried food – this is healthier than using animal fat. Not a lot of red meat or dairy products like butter and eggs are eaten. Scientific research shows that a diet with this balance of food helps people to live long, healthy lives.

In northern European countries like Finland and Sweden, people have one of the world's healthiest diets: a Nordic diet. It includes roasted or stewed reindeer meat, berries, fish, vegetables and rye bread. Reindeer move about freely outside so their meat is low in fat and high in protein. A lot of boiled or steamed cabbage is eaten. Like most vegetables, cabbage has got a lot of vitamins and minerals but very few calories and almost no fat.

## Speaking

**10** Work in pairs. Do the health quiz together. Check your answers on page 91.

### Health Quiz

1 What are green vegetables high in?
 a) carbohydrates  b) calories  c) vitamins
2 Which food has got the least cholesterol in it?
 a) an egg  b) cheese  c) butter
3 Which isn't a good source of calcium?
 a) milk  b) salmon  c) beef
4 What's a good source of iron for a vegetarian?
 a) spinach  b) bananas  c) yoghurt
5 How many of a day's calories does your brain use?
 a) 1–10%  b) 20–30%  c) 50–60%
6 Which snack gives you the most protein?
 a) nuts  b) apples  c) chocolate

**7** Look at the Word Builder. Complete it with words from the text.

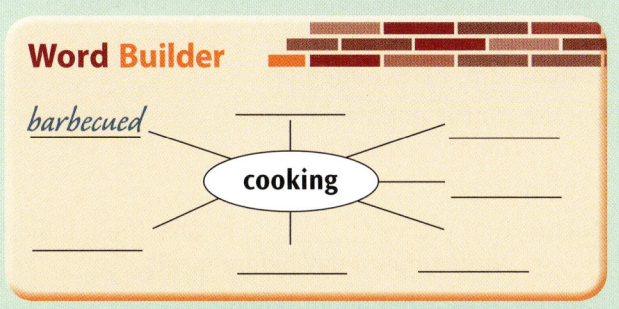

### Word Builder

*barbecued*

cooking

**8** Work in pairs. Write examples of food cooked in each of the ways in the Word Builder.

*barbecued chicken*

▶ Word Bank, page 107

**9** Look at the Key Words from the text. Use them to complete the sentences below.

**Key Words:** Nutrition

calories  carbohydrates  minerals  proteins  vitamins

1 _____ measure the amount of energy in food.
2 _____ are important for your body. For example, calcium helps to build strong bones.
3 _____ in fruit and vegetables help your immune system.
4 _____ in starchy foods give us energy.
5 _____ help to build strong muscles.

## PROJECT

### A survey

**1** Write three questions.

*What do you eat for snacks?*
*How much fresh fruit and vegetables do you eat?*
*How often do you eat sweets?*

**2** Ask other students your questions and write down their answers.

**3** Write a report of your results, like this:

For my survey, I asked thirty-two students in my school questions about their eating habits. These are the results:

First, most students do not eat healthy snacks. Over ninety per cent eat things like cakes, crisps or sweets. Less than ten per cent eat healthy snacks, such as peanuts or fruit.

Secondly, only ten per cent of students eat two or more pieces of fruit per day. About fifty per cent of students only have two or three portions of fruit and vegetables per day ...

**4** Read each other's reports. Do any results surprise you? How well do the students eat?

37

# Study Corner 3

## Language Check

**1 Complete the words in the sentences.**

1 He doesn't sleep well; he suffers from i _ _ _ _ _ _ _ _ .
2 I have to take these t _ _ _ _ _ _ _ twice a day.
3 I've got a terrible h _ _ _ _ _ _ _ .
4 A _ _ _ _ _ _ _ _ _ _ _ is a traditional Chinese treatment.
5 I've got a p _ _ _ in my arm.

**2 Complete the gaps with the words in the box.**

| antibacterial   uncomfortable |
| unlikely   unlucky   unpleasant |

6 She's very _____ , she broke her right arm just before the exams.
7 Yuk! This cough medicine tastes very _____ .
8 The doctor gave me an _____ cream for the cut on my foot.
9 This rain is _____ to stop. Look at the sky!
10 My feet hurt! My new shoes are so _____ !

Vocabulary ☐ / 10

**3 Rewrite the sentences in the passive.**

11 The doctor gave me an injection for my allergy. *I* _____
12 Chocolate doesn't cause spots. *Spots* _____
13 The disease killed over two million people. *Over* _____
14 Some people in Asia eat dogs. *Dogs* _____
15 They took him to hospital after the dog bit him. *He* _____

**4 Put the verbs in brackets in the passive.**

Millions of aspirins [16]_____ (take) every year by people all around the world. The drug [17]_____ (find) in the leaves of the willow tree. They [18]_____ (discover) to be good for pain by the Greek doctor Hippocrates in about 400 BC. The pill, aspirin, [19]_____ (develop) by the German chemist, Felix Hoffman, in 1899. Nowadays, it [20]_____ (use) for everything from headaches and flu to stopping heart attacks.

Glass [21]_____ (produce) for the first time in Egypt in 2,500 BC and the first pair of glasses [22]_____ (made) in Italy in the thirteenth century. The idea for contact lenses [23]_____ (think) of by Leonardo da Vinci in 1508, but the first lenses [24]_____ (not invent) until 1887. Now, lenses or glasses [25]_____ (wear) by over sixty per cent of Americans.

Grammar ☐ / 15

**5 Complete the gaps with one word.**

**Doctor** What can I do for you?
**Patient** I've got a [26]_____ of a sore throat.
**Doctor** Let me take your [27]_____ . It's 38° – that's high.
**Patient** Mm, I feel quite hot.
**Doctor** You've got a cold. You [28]_____ drink plenty of fruit juice.
**Patient** Right.
**Doctor** And you've [29]_____ to take these tablets three times a day before meals.
**Patient** Okay. What about school?
**Doctor** Well, you [30]_____ go to school for a couple of days.
**Patient** Can you give me a note for my teacher?
**Doctor** Yes, sure.

Key Expressions ☐ / 5

## Feedback

🔊 2.14
- Listen and check your answers to the Language Check. Write down your scores.
- Look at the table. Check where you made mistakes.

| Wrong answers: | Look again at: |
| --- | --- |
| Numbers 1–5 | Get Ready – Key Words<br>Unit 9 – Key Words |
| Numbers 6–10 | Unit 8 – Word Builder |
| Numbers 11–25 | Unit 7 – Grammar |
| Numbers 26–30 | Unit 9 – Key Expressions |

- Now do the exercises in Language Check 3 of the Workbook.

## Study Help: Storing words/expressions

Write new and important words and expressions in your notebook.

Mark the main stress in words: <u>head</u>ache

Mark the stressed word(s) in expressions: <u>What</u> can I <u>do</u> for you?

Write important words and expressions in an example sentence.

*Do you do much <u>physical exercise</u> like walking or sport?*

- Do the above for five new words or expressions in this module.

# Module 4

- Talk about personality, relationships and being a teenager; roleplay phone calls.
- Read about teenage problems and families.
- Listen to phone calls.
- Write short emails to friends.
- Learn more about modal verbs and personal pronouns.

# People

## Get Ready

**1** Look at the Key Words and the photos. What do you think the people are like?

> **Key Words:** Personality Adjectives
>
> easy-going  energetic  extroverted  friendly  hard-working  helpful  honest  independent  introverted  kind  lazy  organised  outgoing  practical  quiet  reliable  sensitive  shy  sociable  talkative  thoughtful  tidy  untidy

*The girl in photo a) looks energetic and outgoing.*

**2** Listen to the people in the photos and check your guesses from Exercise 1.

**3** Listen again and answer the questions.
1. What after-school activities does Jenny do?
2. Why does Scott help his neighbour go shopping?
3. What are Robert's interests?
4. What is Lisa's hobby?

**4** Work in pairs. Ask your partner the questions and then look at the results on page 91. Is the personality description accurate for you?

## How Extrovert Are You?

Do these statements describe you?
Mark each one on a scale of 1–4.

1 – no, not at all  2 – sometimes
3 – often  4 – yes, definitely.

| | | |
|---|---|---|
| 1 | When I'm out with my friends, I talk less than the others. | 1 2 3 4 |
| 2 | I listen to other people before I give my opinions. | 1 2 3 4 |
| 3 | When I go to a party, I only talk to people I know. | 1 2 3 4 |
| 4 | I am a thoughtful, careful and loyal person. | 1 2 3 4 |
| 5 | When I'm busy and the phone rings, I ignore it. | 1 2 3 4 |

39

# 10 Problem Page

## Warm-up

**1** Look at the Key Words. Which words are positive and which are negative? Use them to describe the people in the photos.

> **Key Words:** Feelings
>
> angry   annoyed   anxious   bored   calm
> cheerful   delighted   depressed   excited
> furious   nervous   relaxed   sad   scared
> thrilled   upset   worried

## Reading

**2** Do you read the advice columns in magazines? Which problems do people often write about?

**3** Read the problem page letters (1–3) and match them with the replies (a–c).

**4** Which problem is the most serious? Why?

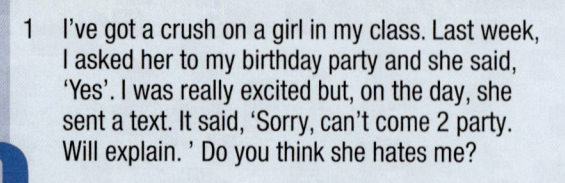

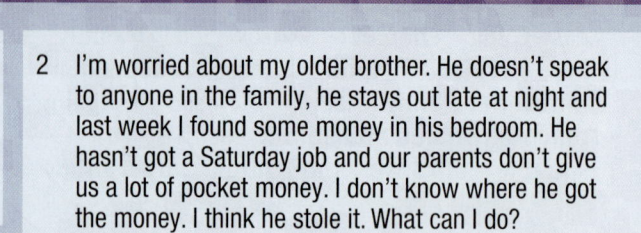

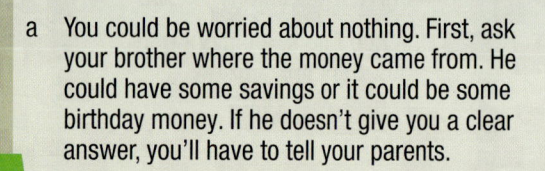

## PROBLEM BUSTERS

**Q**

1 I've got a crush on a girl in my class. Last week, I asked her to my birthday party and she said, 'Yes'. I was really excited but, on the day, she sent a text. It said, 'Sorry, can't come 2 party. Will explain.' Do you think she hates me?

2 I'm worried about my older brother. He doesn't speak to anyone in the family, he stays out late at night and last week I found some money in his bedroom. He hasn't got a Saturday job and our parents don't give us a lot of pocket money. I don't know where he got the money. I think he stole it. What can I do?

**A**

a You could be worried about nothing. First, ask your brother where the money came from. He could have some savings or it could be some birthday money. If he doesn't give you a clear answer, you'll have to tell your parents.

b This girl is a very clever bully and she is controlling all of you. Talk honestly to your old friends – they can't be happy with the situation either. Show that good friends talk to each other and solve their problems. Remember, there must be a reason why she is a bully so try to be kind – but don't let her split up your friendships.

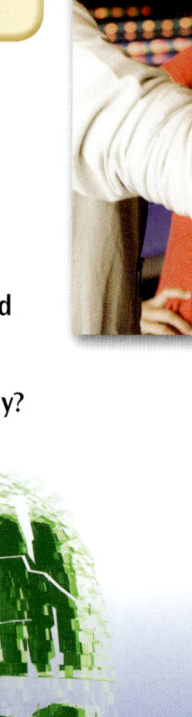

40

## Grammar: Speculating

**5** Complete the sentences from the text with modal verbs for speculating: *must*, *could* and *can't*.

1 They _____ be happy with the situation either.
2 She _____ like you.
3 He _____ have some savings.

**6** Match the modal verbs (1–3) with the meanings (a–c).

| 1 must | a) I'm sure it's not true. (strong evidence) |
| --- | --- |
| 2 could | b) I'm sure it's true. (strong evidence) |
| 3 can't | c) Perhaps it's true. (weak evidence) |

## Practice

**7** Complete the speculations about people with *must* or *can't*.

1 Look, she's smiling and laughing. She _can't_ be angry.
2 Sam's had a terrible argument with his girlfriend. He _____ be upset.
3 They're flying to Alaska on Saturday. They _____ be excited.
4 She's a bully and she's very unpleasant. She _____ have a lot of friends.
5 My brother's most important exam is tomorrow. He _____ be feeling anxious.
6 Sally _____ be a nervous person – she loves dangerous sports and horror films.

3 There's a new girl in our class this term. At first, we all liked her because she's very generous. Now, she's making a lot of trouble: she talks about people and causes arguments. Last term, we were all good friends but now we're in small groups and we don't know who our friends are. It's horrible!

c No, that can't be the reason. Think about it: she must like you because she accepted your invitation and she sent you a text to apologise. Next time you see her, be friendly and relaxed. It'll be okay!

**8** Look at a social network profile. Complete the sentences with *must*, *can't* and *could*.

**MY PROFILE**    updates    pics    logout

**Friends:** 3
**Interests:** football, basketball, tennis, swimming
**Favourite music:** –
**Favourite time:** nine o'clock on Monday morning!
**Favourite food:** pasta, pizza – anything Italian!
**Favourite drink:** black coffee

+ add as friend
✉ send message

1 She _could_ be very sociable.
2 She _____ like sport.
3 She _____ like music.
4 She _____ enjoy school.
5 She _____ be Italian.

**9** Look at another social network profile. Make sentences about the person using *must*, *can't* and *could*.

*He must like music.*

**MY PROFILE**    updates    pics    logout

**Friends:** 526
**Interests:** drawing, painting, photography
**Favourite music:** Seal, Jay-Z, Red Hot Chili Peppers, Alicia Keys
**Favourite time:** four o'clock on Friday afternoon
**Favourite food:** fish and chips, bacon sandwiches, curry – all traditional British food
**Favourite drink:** tea with three sugars

+ add as friend
✉ send message

## Your Turn

**10 Game** Think of a friend. Describe him/her to your partner. Give one clue at a time. Your partner must guess the person.

A *He's in our class.*
B *It could be Tomas.*
A *He's shy.*
B *It can't be Tomas! It could be Danny.*
A *No. He speaks French at home.*
B *It must be Etienne.*
A *That's right.*

**TIMEOUT!** ▶ Page 96, Exercise 10

# 11 Generation Gap

## Warm-up

**1** Which of the things below do you argue about with your parents?
- homework • clothes • bedroom
- playing computer games • watching TV
- hairstyle • friends • mobile phone
- making phone calls at home • getting home late
- doing household chores • playing music too loud
- having a tattoo or body piercing

## Reading

**2** Read the text about family arguments. Which of the things in Exercise 1 do the family argue about?

## The kids speak

**Edward:**
Mum and Dad think I'm a little boy and it's really annoying. I mean, I'm nearly sixteen and they won't let me have an earring or a tattoo. We argue a lot about my clothes. The other BIG problem is homework. They make me do it every day and won't allow me to go out until it's finished. I didn't do well in maths last year so they make me take extra classes after school.

**Sophie:**
I love my mum and dad but we argue about some things. Dad makes a fuss when I spend more than five minutes in the bathroom and he gets angry when I use all the hot water. Mum gets annoyed when I won't make my bed or do the washing-up. They say I make phone calls all the time but that's not true – I usually send texts. Anyway, they won't allow me to take my phone to bed so I can't send texts at night. That isn't fair, is it?

## The parents speak

**Pete and Clare Atkins:**
We're very proud of Edward and Sophie. They both make friends easily so they've got busy social lives. On school nights we make them do their homework before we let them see their friends.

Edward is becoming very independent but he's only fifteen so he needs our support and advice. He wants an earring but we think he's too young to make that choice. We'll make him wait until he's eighteen – and we'll make him pay for it from his own money! When he makes an effort, Edward does well at school.

Sophie does her best at school too and, luckily, she always does her homework without an argument. Sometimes she's a bit cheeky but she's very funny and she makes us laugh. She spends hours in the bathroom doing her hair and trying on make-up. Also, she makes a terrible mess in her bedroom – there's always an argument when we make her tidy it! She makes hundreds of phone calls every day so she always wants pocket money to buy credit. She makes money babysitting and doing housework for our neighbours.

**Skills**

**3** Which person from the text could say these things?
1. I don't like doing homework. *Edward*
2. There's no hot water!
3. It's not fair! All my friends have got earrings.
4. Yes, I'll look after your children on Friday evening.
5. Make your bed and tidy your room!

**4** Look at the Word Builder. Find the words in the box in the text and add them to the Word Builder.

> my/your bed   a fuss   a mess   an effort   friends
> homework   housework   money   phone calls
> someone laugh   the washing-up   well
> my/your hair   my/your best

**Word Builder**

| make | *your bed* |
|---|---|
| do | *homework* |

**5** Verb Quiz Complete the expressions with *make* or *do*.
1. *do* the shopping
2. ___ a cup of tea
3. ___ a suggestion
4. ___ trouble
5. ___ a mistake
6. ___ athletics
7. ___ puzzles
8. ___ calculations

▶ Word Bank, page 109

**6** Complete the text with the correct form of *make* or *do*.

> When I get home from school, I ¹___ a cup of tea. Then, I go to my room and I ²___ my bed. After that, I ³___ my homework – my parents ⁴___ a fuss when I don't. We get a lot of homework and you have to ⁵___ an effort to ⁶___ well. I worry about my marks but my parents always say, 'Just work hard and ⁷___ your best.'

**7** Look at the Sentence Builder. Find more examples of the verbs in the text.

**Sentence Builder**

| They | **make** | me | take extra classes. |
|---|---|---|---|
| We | **let** | them | see their friends at the weekends |
| We | **'ll make** | him | wait until he's eighteen. |

**8** Look at the example.

*They won't let me have an earring.*

Find two more examples in the text of *won't* with the meaning 'refuse to do something'.

**9** Rewrite the sentences using *make* or *let*.
1. In sports lessons, we have to warm-up first.
   Our games teacher *makes us warm-up first.*
2. My parents say I can't go to rock concerts.
   My parents won't ___
3. I have to tidy my room at weekends.
   My parents ___
4. They had to stay in at break.
   Their teacher ___
5. I can use the Internet on my dad's computer.
   My dad ___

**Speaking**

**10** Look at the expressions from two arguments. Who says them? A teenager (T) or a parent (P)?
1. ☐ Where have you been?
2. ☐ Can I have a …? Why not?
3. ☐ Oh, please. I just want a small one on my shoulder.
4. ☐ Why are you late?
5. ☐ Why didn't you phone home?
6. ☐ It's not fair. All my friends have got them.
7. ☐ You never listen to me.
8. ☐ Everyone else stays out late.
9. ☐ I'll pay for it with my own money.
10. ☐ You're too young to have a …

**11** Work in pairs. Roleplay two situations.

▶ Student A, page 89
▶ Student B, page 90

**Fact or Fiction?**
Sixty-six per cent of American parents say they have the same values as their children. Only forty-six per cent of teenagers say they have the same values as their parents!
— Answer on page 92. —

**TIMEOUT!** ▶ Page 96, Exercise 11

## 12 In Town

### Warm-up

**1** Work in pairs. What is happening in the photo?

### Reading and Listening

**2** Read and listen to the dialogue. Check your guesses from Exercise 1.

*Gwen, Sam and Jasmin go into town on their free afternoon.*

**Gwen** Hey, there's a good film on at six o'clock with Kirsten Dunst.
**Sam** Let's phone Matt.
**Gwen** Hasn't he got a headache? Anyway, his mobile's not working.
**Jasmin** No problem. I'll ring the school.
**Sam** That's a good idea.
**Mr B** Petergate School.
**Jasmin** Hello. Mr Bywater? It's Jasmin. Can I speak to Matt, please?
**Mr B** Hello, Jasmin. Hold on a moment. I'll see if he's here. Sorry, he's not in his room. Can I take a message?
**Jasmin** Yes, please. Can you ask him to phone me?
**Mr B** What's your number?
**Jasmin** It's 07381 776098.
**Mr B** Just a moment. So that's 07381 776098.
**Jasmin** Okay, thanks, Mr Bywater.
**Mr B** Not at all, Jasmin. Bye.

*Twenty minutes later, Matt calls Jasmin.*

**Jasmin** Hi, Matt!
**Matt** Hi, my cell phone is okay now. I got your message.
**Jasmin** Right. Do you want to go to the Riverside Cinema with us tonight?
**Matt** Sorry, I can't. I'd like to but I'm still not feeling great.
**Jasmin** Come on, we're not going without you. You need to get out a bit. Kirsten Dunst is in the film. You love her!
**Matt** I don't know. Anyway, the Riverside's miles away.
**Jasmin** No, it's not. It's only ten minutes from school.
**Matt** Hang on, let me look at the map. Oh, all right. I'll be there in about twenty minutes.
**Jasmin** Great. See you!

**3** Read the dialogue again and answer the questions.
1 Who doesn't want to ring up Matt?
2 Why do they have to phone the school?
3 Why does Jasmin think Matt will like the film?
4 What reasons does Matt give for not going?

# Skills

## Speaking

**4** Look at the Key Expressions and answer the questions.

1. Which phone call (1 or 2) is more formal?
2. What three expressions mean 'wait'?
3. In call (1), why does Jasmin say *It's Jasmin* but in call (2) Matt doesn't say *It's Matt*?

### Key Expressions: Phone Calls

| 1 | 2 |
|---|---|
| **A** Hello. Mr Bywater? **It's Jasmin. Can I speak to Matt, please?** | **A** Hi, Matt! |
| **B** **Hold on a moment.** I'll see if he's here. **Sorry, he's not in his room. Can I take a message?** | **B** Hi, my cell phone is okay now. **I got your message.** |
| **A** Yes, please. **Can you ask him to phone me?** | **A** Right. **Do you want to** go to the Riverside Cinema? |
| **B** What's your number? | **B** Sorry, I can't. I'd like to but I'm still not feeling great. |
| **A** It's 07381 776098. | **A** Come on. |
| **B** **Just a moment.** So that's 07381 776098. | **B** **Hang on** … Oh, all right. I'll be there … |
| **A** Okay, thanks, Mr Bywater. | **A** Great. See you! |
| **B** Not at all, Jasmin. Bye. | |

**5** Work in pairs. Act out phone call 1. Take turns to phone a friend's house and leave a message with the friend's mother or father.

**6** Write notes about one of these things to do in town this weekend. Think about where to meet and what time.

- watch a film
- go to a party
- go bowling
- go shopping
- go to a concert
- have a meal

*watch a film / Odeon Cinema / 6 p.m. Saturday*

**7** Work in pairs. Act out phone call 2.

▶ Student A, page 89
▶ Student B, page 90

## Everyday Listening 🔊

**1** Look at the Listening Help.

### Listening Help: Specific information

- Before you listen, look at the questions and read any texts you have to complete (e.g. messages, notices, leaflets).
- Guess what kind of information you need (e.g. times, prices, names, dates).
- When the CD is playing, listen for this kind of information.
- Remember, you can say the same thing in different ways (e.g. *movie/film, half-past three/three thirty*).

**2.22** **2** Listen to the phone conversations. Use the Listening Help to help to complete the messages.

> Chris
> Tom called. He wants to go to the ¹_____ on ²_____ afternoon. Phone him at his ³_____ house. Her number is ⁴_____.
> Mum x

> Kirsty
> Cathy phoned. Meet her outside the ⁵_____ at ⁶_____ this afternoon. Take the new Coldplay ⁷_____. She wants to go to Gino's for an ⁸_____.
> Dad

**2.23** **3** **Listen closely** Listen and underline the sentence you hear, a or b.

1. a) He's not here at the moment.
   b) He isn't here at the moment.
2. a) And my mobile's not working.
   b) And my mobile isn't working.
3. a) Sorry, Cathy, she's not in.
   b) Sorry, Cathy, she isn't in.
4. a) We're not sure.
   b) We aren't sure.
5. a) No, they're not going out now.
   b) No, they aren't going out now.

**2.24** **4** Listen again and repeat the sentences.

**TIMEOUT!** ▶ Page 97, Exercise 12

45

## Your Challenge

### Writing: Emails

**1** Read the emails (a–e) and put them in order.

**a**
from Jamie
to Vicky
subject Saturday

Great! See you then!
Jamie

**b**
from Vicky
to Jamie
subject Saturday

Jamie,
Thanks for the email. I'd love to come but I can't. Unfortunately, I've got a dentist's appointment at eleven. Some other time maybe.
Vicky

**c**
from Vicky
to Jamie
subject Saturday

Hi J,
That's a good idea. I can meet you all outside the dentist's then. By the way, Laura can come! Luckily, she hasn't got her tennis class this Saturday. She lives near the dentist's so she can meet us there. See you on Saturday!
Vicky

**d**
from Jamie
to Vicky
subject Saturday

Vicky,
We don't have to go there at eleven. We can go a bit later. Half eleven? Actually, we could wait for you outside the dentist's, if you like. By the way, can you tell Laura? Maybe she wants to come, too.

**e**
from Jamie
to Vicky
subject Saturday

Hi there Vicky,
Paul and I are going to the new amusement park on Saturday. My older sister's got the car and she can take us there at about eleven. How about coming with us? It isn't too expensive because there's a special offer for the first month. Anyway, send me reply or phone me.
Jamie

### Text Builder

**2** Look at the words in red. What do they refer to?

*1  then – eleven thirty*

1  then (c)        4  she (e)
2  there (c)       5  us (e)
3  there (d)       6  it (e)

**3** Look at the words in blue. Which of the words mean:

1  It's a pity but …
2  Oh, another thing …
3  In fact, …
4  It's lucky because …
5  I want to change the subject.

**4** Write notes to make arrangements for this weekend. Use the blue linking words from the emails.

**STEP 1** Work in pairs. Each person writes a short note to their partner to suggest going out this weekend.

#### Writing Help: Checking
- Read the instructions again. Have you completed the task?
- Have you used the correct tenses and linking words?
- Have you checked spelling and punctuation?

**STEP 2** Look at the Writing Help before you give your note.

**STEP 3** Reply to the notes. You would love to come but can't because you have got something on.

**STEP 4** Reply and suggest another time or day.

**STEP 5** Reply and agree to go out with your partner.

**5** **Speak Out** Tell the class about your arrangement.

*Steve and I agreed to go to the cinema at six o'clock on Saturday.*

# Understanding Grammar: Personal pronouns

**1** Complete the table.

| Subject pronouns *I like John.* | Object pronouns *Jim likes me.* | Possessive adjectives *This is my pen.* | Possessive pronouns *It's mine* | Reflexive pronouns *I cut myself.* |
|---|---|---|---|---|
| I | me | my | ¹ _mine_ | myself |
| you | you | ² _____ | yours | yourself |
| he | ³ _____ | his | his | himself |
| she | her | ⁴ _____ | hers | herself |
| it | it | its | – | itself |
| we | ⁵ _____ | our | ours | ourselves |
| you | you | your | ⁶ _____ | yourselves |
| they | them | their | theirs | themselves |

**2** Complete the text with pronouns and possessive adjectives from the table.

Jovana and I are best friends. ¹_____ went to primary school together. ²_____ parents are friends, too – ³_____ mother and ⁴_____ mother were at university together. Jovana is living in New York now – ⁵_____ went there with ⁶_____ parents six months ago. ⁷_____ are diplomats and ⁸_____ often work abroad. Usually, ⁹_____ take ¹⁰_____ children with ¹¹_____ . Jovana loves New York, ¹²_____ parks, cafés and busy life. ¹³_____ father is interested in art so ¹⁴_____ often takes ¹⁵_____ to museums and galleries. ¹⁶_____ has a new boyfriend, Jerry. Last week Jovana sent ¹⁷_____ a letter with a photo of ¹⁸_____ . ¹⁹_____ is very good-looking. Jovana is coming home for Christmas. ²⁰_____ 'll definitely meet up!

## Reflexive pronouns

**3** Read the sentences and match the words (1–2) with the people (a–b).

Jovana has a Christmas present for Anna. She bought ¹**her** a nice scarf. She bought ²**herself** new gloves.

a) Anna   b) Jovana

**4** Complete the sentences with the correct object pronoun or reflexive pronoun.

1 We didn't know Claire so she introduced _____ .
2 They are so selfish, they always think only about _____ .
3 My sister was hungry so I made _____ a sandwich.
4 You're all dirty. Just look at _____ in the mirror.
5 My home town is beautiful, I love _____ .
6 My father cut _____ when he was building a bookshelf.
7 When Mike arrived, we introduced _____ to the other guests.
8 Last night, we saw Jill on TV. They filmed _____ in a supermarket.

## Reflexive and reciprocal pronouns

**5** Look at the sentences (1–2) and match them with the pictures (a–b).

1 Jerry and Jovana are looking at **each other**. They are in love.
2 Jerry and Jovana are preparing for a date. They are looking at **themselves** in the mirror.

a

b

**6** Complete the sentences with the correct words.

1 Anna and Jovana often phone *each other/themselves*.
2 Anna and Jovana describe *each other/themselves* as 'best friends'.

**7** Complete the sentences with *each other, ourselves, yourselves* or *themselves*.

1 We don't know _____ very well but we like _____ a lot.
2 If you two are hungry, go and get _____ some lunch.
3 Jovana and Anna write emails to _____ once a week.
4 The film was good – we really enjoyed _____ .
5 We kissed _____ for the first time at a party.
6 Film stars can read about _____ in magazines.

47

# Study Corner 4

## Language Check

**1 Complete the words in the sentences.**

Sue is a ¹ s _ _ _ _ _ _ _ _ girl and makes friends easily.
Pat is very ² e _ _ _ _ - _ _ _ _ _ . She never gets ³ w _ _ _ _ _ _ about exams.
Carl is quite ⁴ s _ _ _ _ _ _ _ _ _ and gets ⁵ u _ _ _ _ when people tease him.

**2 Choose the correct word.**

6 My parents never *do / make* a fuss.
7 I don't *do / make* many phone calls; I prefer to send text messages.
8 My sister always *does / makes* well at maths.
9 My mum got angry because I *did / made* a mess in the kitchen.
10 My teacher says I should *do / make* more effort in sport.

Vocabulary ☐ / 10

**3 Choose the best alternative in each sentence.**

11 Rose talks about Ivan all the time. She *can't / must* fancy him.
12 Elena is always friendly and outgoing. She *can't / could* be shy.
13 Tomas and Oliver are always together. They *could / must* be good friends.
14 Kathy's in a bad mood today. She *could / can't* be worried about something.
15 Neil plays tennis, football and basketball. He *could / must* be athletic.

**4 Complete the sentences with the correct form of *make* or *let*.**

16 My parents _____ me tidy my bedroom last night.
17 Their school _____ students leave their mobiles switched off.
18 Her parents will _____ her wait until she's eighteen to get a tattoo.
19 Mum and Dad won't _____ me have a TV in my bedroom.
20 'I'll _____ you have an earring when you are older.'

**5 Complete the gaps with pronouns.**

She looked at ²¹_____ in the mirror and then turned to Tom. They smiled at each ²²_____ and laughed. 'Do you remember when we met ²³_____ other outside the bus station?' she asked. 'Of course I do,' said Tom. 'I thought you were talking to ²⁴_____ but you were on your mobile phone! Then, when we looked at ²⁵_____ other, we knew it was love at first sight!'

Grammar ☐ / 15

**6 Complete the gaps with one word.**

A Hello.
B Hi, Mrs Smith. ²⁶_____'s Joanna Johnson. ²⁷_____ I speak to Sue, please?
A ²⁸_____ on, I'll get her. ²⁹_____ , she's not in at the moment. Can I ³⁰_____ a message?
B Thanks. Can you ask her to …

Communication ☐ / 5

## Feedback

🔊 2.25
• Listen and check your answers to the Language Check. Write down your scores.
• Look at the table below. Check where you made mistakes.

| Wrong answers: | Look again at: |
| --- | --- |
| Numbers 1–5 | Get Ready and Unit 10 – Key Words |
| Numbers 6–10 | Unit 11 – Word Builder |
| Numbers 11–15 | Unit 10 – Grammar |
| Numbers 16–20 | Unit 11 – Sentence Builder |
| Numbers 21–25 | Understanding Grammar |
| Numbers 26–30 | Unit 12 – Key Expressions |

• Now do the exercises in Language Check 4 of the Workbook.

## Study Help: Memorising vocabulary

How do you remember words? What kind of learner are you?

• **Visual**. You look at new words. You cover the page and try to 'see' the words in your mind. Sometimes you draw pictures next to words in your vocabulary book.
• **Oral**. You repeat words to yourself (silently or aloud) again and again.
• **Analytical**. You break words into different parts and think how they fit together (e.g. skate + board). You think about differences and similarities between English words and words in your language (e.g. tourist, turista (Spanish)).

• Look at Key Words boxes in Modules 1–4. Learn five new words. Ask your partner to test you.

# Module 5

- Talk about travel and make suggestions.
- Read about safaris and nomads.
- Listen to travel plans.
- Write a description of a tour round your country.
- Learn more about the Present Perfect.

# On the Move

## Get Ready

**1** Look at the Key Words. Add five more types of transport.

> **Key Words: Transport**
>
> **Go by:** campervan   canoe   coach   dinghy   helicopter   jeep   jet ski   lorry   motorbike   mountain bike   plane   snowmobile   tram   underground (metro)   van   yacht
> **Go on:** foot   horseback

**2** Which types of transport do we use for fun?

**3** Work in pairs. Ask and answer the questions.
1. Which types of transport do you use?
2. Which do you use every day?
3. Which would you like to try?
4. Which would you never use?

**4** Listen to four people. Who:
1. had an accident?   ☐ and ☐
2. takes part in competitions?   ☐ and ☐
3. shares their interest with their boyfriend/girlfriend?   ☐ and ☐
4. does their hobby at weekends?   ☐ and ☐
5. started it two years ago?   ☐ and ☐

**5** **Speak Out** Do you agree with these statements? Say why or why not. Tell the class.
- People in my town drive too fast.
- Young people on motorbikes are dangerous.
- Extreme sports fans are crazy!

49

# 13 TV Traveller

## Warm-up

**1** Look at the Key Words and decide which people have to travel a lot.

**Key Words: Jobs**

farmer   fashion model   film maker
flight attendant   photographer   police officer
politician   secretary   tour guide   travel writer
TV presenter

*Farmers don't have to travel a lot. They work on their land.*

**2** Look at the photos of Clara Saruhashi. What does she do?

## Reading

**3** Read the text. Check your guesses from Exercise 2.

**4** Read the text again. Are the sentences true (T), false (F) or is there no information (NI)?

1. ☐ Clara Saruhashi travels a lot.
2. ☐ She enjoys her job.
3. ☐ She became interested in travelling at university.
4. ☐ Most of her work is in a TV studio.
5. ☐ Her husband always travels with her.
6. ☐ Camping in the Amazon jungle was a good experience.

Have you ever canoed along the Amazon River? Or travelled across the Sahara desert on a camel? I haven't! But Clara Saruhashi, a TV presenter, has done both – and a lot more! Clara's job with UTravel TV takes her all over the world and she has made more than a hundred programmes.

When I interviewed her, I asked, 'What have you done in the last six months?' She answered, 'I've done some really interesting things: I have walked on the Great Wall of China, I've climbed Machu Picchu in Peru and I've swum with dolphins. I love being close to animals so it was a fantastic experience!'

My next question: 'When did you become interested in travelling?' Her answer, 'I have never wanted a safe job in an office. When I was a little girl, I wanted to be a flight attendant or a tour guide. I studied languages at university so I could travel. I'm very lucky: I go to amazing places, meet fascinating people – and I get paid for it!'

Clara has already been to six continents but there is one place she hasn't visited. 'I haven't been to Antarctica yet but I really want to go. I've read lots of books about the area and I think it will be a fantastic experience. The problem is, I hate being cold!'

I had a final question. 'Have you ever been in danger?' Clara laughed and said, 'There was a giant spider in my tent in the Amazon jungle – it wasn't dangerous but I was very frightened. I've never liked spiders!'

## Grammar: Present Perfect

**5** Complete the sentences from the text with the verbs in the Present Perfect.

| Past event | Present consequence |
|---|---|
| She _____ more than a hundred programmes. → | She is a well-known TV presenter. |
| I _____ lots of books about the area. → | She knows a lot about Antarctica. |

**6** Do we know when exactly the past events in Exercise 5 happened?

**7** Read the sentences. Translate the words in **bold** into your language.
1. Have you **ever** been in danger?
2. I have **never** wanted a safe job in an office.
3. She has **already** been to six continents.
4. I haven't been to Antarctica **yet**.
5. Has she been to Peru **yet**?

**8** Match the words (1–4) with the types of sentences (a–d). One of the words goes with two types.

*1 – b*

| 1 | already | a) | questions |
| 2 | yet | b) | affirmative sentences |
| 3 | ever | c) | negative sentences with *not* |
| 4 | never | d) | negative sentences without *not* |

## Practice

**9** Use the correct verbs in the box in the Present Perfect to make affirmative and negative sentences about Clara Saruhashi's career.

| camp | ~~make~~ | present | ride | study |
| swim | visit | | | |

*She has made a lot of TV programmes.*
- a lot of TV programmes (✓)
- sharks (✗)
- French, Spanish and Italian (✓)
- in the Amazon jungle (✓)
- an elephant (✗)
- programmes about cooking (✗)
- the South Pole (✗)

**10** Read the interview with a travel writer. Choose the correct words to complete the sentences and put them in the correct places.

A Have you been to China? (never / (yet))
*Have you been to China yet?*
B Yes, I've been there three times. (already / ever)
A Have you seen a wild panda? (ever / already)
B No, I've seen a wild panda. (never / ever).
And I haven't seen one in a zoo. (never / yet).

**11** Read the travel writer's plans for his next trip. Make sentences with *already* and *yet*.

*He's already applied for a new passport.*
*He hasn't booked a hotel in Budapest yet.*

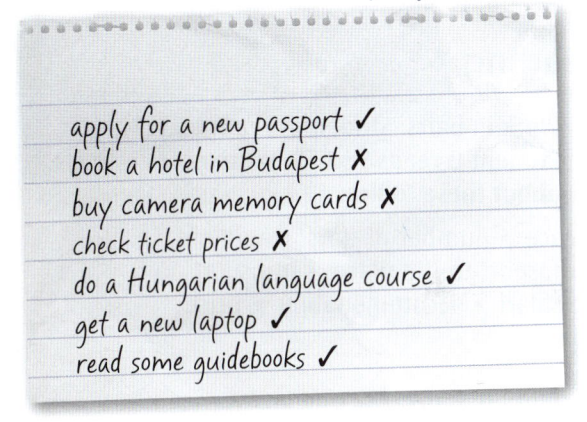

> apply for a new passport ✓
> book a hotel in Budapest ✗
> buy camera memory cards ✗
> check ticket prices ✗
> do a Hungarian language course ✓
> get a new laptop ✓
> read some guidebooks ✓

**12 Game** Cover the list in Exercise 11. Ask and answer about the travel writer's plans.

*Has he applied for a new passport yet? Yes, he has.*
*Has he booked a hotel in Budapest yet? No, he hasn't.*

## Your Turn

**13** Pair work. Ask and answer questions.
▶ Student A, page 89
▶ Student B, page 90

**14** **Speak Out** Tell the class two things about your partner.

*Marta has been abroad. She has never travelled by ship.*

**15** Use the cues below and *already*, *yet* and *never* to make sentences about what you have and haven't done in your life. Add your own ideas.

- try bungee jumping • swim in the sea
- take part in a sports competition • go abroad
- climb the highest mountain in my country
- go on holidays on my own • learn to drive
- finish school

*I've already been abroad three times.*
*I haven't finished school yet.*

**TIMEOUT!** ▶ Page 98, Exercise 13

51

## 14 On Safari

### Warm-up

1  Look at the Key Words. Which five animals are not from Africa? What other African animals can you add to the list?

**Key Words:** Animals

antelope   baboon   buffalo
cheetah   giraffe   hippo   hyena
kangaroo   koala   leopard   panda
polar bear   python   rhino   tiger
wildebeest (or 'gnu')   zebra

### Reading

2  Work in pairs. Student A reads text (1). Student B reads text (2). Write notes about these topics:

• place  • number of days  • animals
• transport to the place  • transport on the safari  • accommodation  • price
• dates

3  Work in pairs. Ask and answer questions about the safaris. Use these question words.

• Where  • How long  • What  • How
• How much  • When

*Where is your safari? What animals can you see?*

4  Work in pairs. Answer the questions.
1  Which safari would you like to go on?
2  What animals would you like to see?
3  What other places would you like to go to?
4  What would you like to see and do there?

5  Look at the Word Builder. Copy and complete it with compound words in blue from the texts. Are they nouns (n) or adjectives (adj.)?

**Word Builder**

| one word | backpacker (n) |
|---|---|
| two words | nature lover (n) |
| two words with hyphen | hard-working (adj.) |

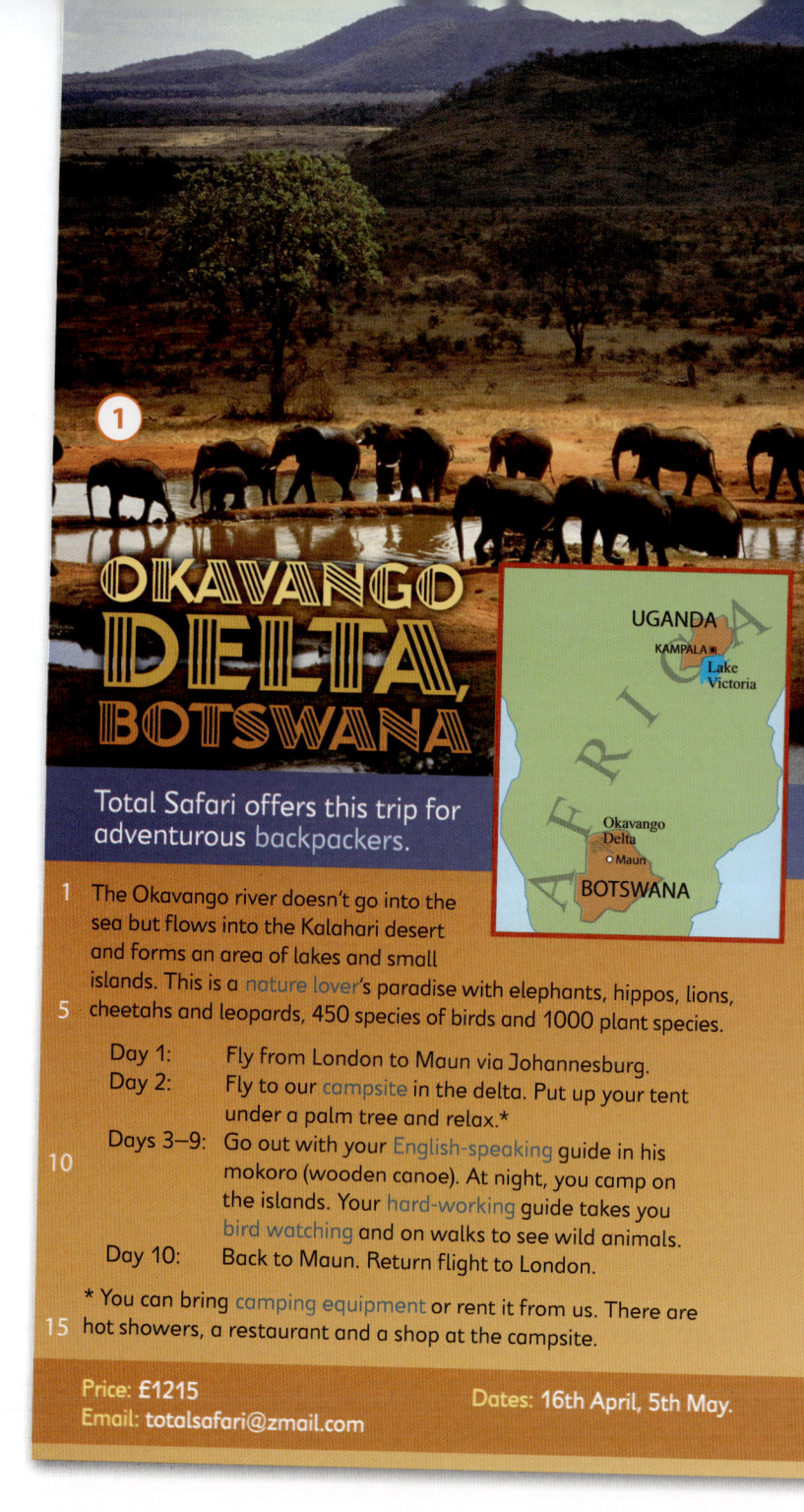

### 1

## OKAVANGO DELTA, BOTSWANA

Total Safari offers this trip for adventurous backpackers.

1  The Okavango river doesn't go into the sea but flows into the Kalahari desert and forms an area of lakes and small islands. This is a nature lover's paradise with elephants, hippos, lions,
5  cheetahs and leopards, 450 species of birds and 1000 plant species.

Day 1:    Fly from London to Maun via Johannesburg.
Day 2:    Fly to our campsite in the delta. Put up your tent under a palm tree and relax.*
Days 3–9: Go out with your English-speaking guide in his
10        mokoro (wooden canoe). At night, you camp on the islands. Your hard-working guide takes you bird watching and on walks to see wild animals.
Day 10:   Back to Maun. Return flight to London.

* You can bring camping equipment or rent it from us. There are
15 hot showers, a restaurant and a shop at the campsite.

Price: £1215
Email: totalsafari@zmail.com
Dates: 16th April, 5th May.

6  Complete the compound words.

**My Daily Blog**

www.mydailyblog.org

Last summer, me and my friends got student rail tickets and travelled round Europe. We went
¹ sight _____ in big cities. We stayed in
² camp _____ or youth hostels – they were not exactly ³ luxury _____ and were full of other
⁴ back _____ with all their ⁵ camping _____ . The rooms weren't ⁶ air-_____ , so sometimes it wasn't very comfortable. We made a lot of new friends as most of the foreign students were
⁷ English-_____ .

# CHIMP AND GORILLA SAFARI, UGANDA

**Do you like watching chimps and gorillas on TV? Come and see them in the wild!**

1 Uganda's national parks are in spectacular rainforests with an incredible variety of wildlife including TEN species of primates. The stars of the show are, of course, the rare mountain gorillas.

5 Day 1: Fly from London to Kampala.
Days 2–5: Track chimpanzees in Kibale National Park.
Days 6–9: Trekking to find gorillas in Bwindi National Park. Watching them is an incredible experience!
10 Days 10–12: Go to a well-known chimp sanctuary on Lake Victoria. Forty-six chimps from zoos and circuses live here. Remember, they're not wild so they love playing!
Day 13: Day in Kampala. Five-star hotel. Do some
15 sightseeing and relaxing.
Day 14: Return flight to London.

All accommodation is in luxury hotels, lodges or campsites. Food is included. Transport by air-conditioned 4x4 vehicles.

20 Price: £3100    Dates: 12th February, 18th June
Email: safari@totem.com

**7 Word Quiz** Find compound words in the word chains.
1 nightlifestyle
2 snowmobilephonebookshelf
3 weekdayschoolholidayresort
4 skateboardingschoollunchtimetabletenniscourt

▶ Word Bank, pages 107–108

**8** Look at the Sentence Builder. In which sentence is *watching* the subject and in which is it the object of the sentence?

---

**Sentence Builder**

1 Do you like **watching** chimps and gorillas?
2 **Watching** them is an incredible experience.

---

## Skills

**9** Write two sentences about each activity in the box. Use these words:
- I love / like / can't stand …
- … is good fun / great / cool / horrible / boring / relaxing.

*I love travelling. Travelling is good fun!*

| travelling   camping   cycling
| swimming   playing football
| studying English   dancing
| going to school   getting up early
| doing my homework

## Speaking

**10** Work in pairs. Ask and answer the questions. Check your scores on page 91.

### How Adventurous Are You?

1 When you go to an amusement park, what do you do?
  a) only go on the slow rides
  b) go on rides but avoid the most scary ones
  c) go on everything!

2 What do you do when you go to the beach?
  a) sunbathe
  b) walk along the beach
  c) swim in the sea on your own

3 How would you like to travel round Europe?
  a) with your family
  b) on a school trip
  c) backpacking with a friend

4 Which of these places would you prefer to spend the night in?
  a) a luxury hotel
  b) a youth hostel
  c) a tent

5 Which of these things would you like to do?
  a) go sightseeing in a big city
  b) try paragliding
  c) go to a summer adventure camp

---

**Fact or Fiction?**
There are only 660 mountain gorillas in the world.
Answer on page 92.

**TIMEOUT!** ▶ Page 98, Exercise 14

# 15 The Boat Trip

## Warm-up

1 Look at the photo. Have you ever been boating or canoeing? Where?

## Reading and Listening

2 Read and listen to the dialogue. Answer the questions.

Which of the characters:
1 have an argument?
2 nearly loses his jacket?
3 suggests getting in the water?
4 suggests calling somebody?
5 gets the jacket?

*The next weekend, the group rent a boat on the Norfolk Broads, an area of lakes and rivers near Norwich.*

**Matt** O sole mio, la la la laaa …
**Gwen** Matt, sit down. Don't be so silly. You're going to sink the boat!
**Matt** Oh, don't be so scared, Gwen. Don't you like my singing?
**Gwen** No, I don't. I'm sick of you being stupid all the time!
**Sam** Come on you two. Just stop arguing.
**Matt** Whoa! I nearly fell in!
**Gwen** Serves you right!
**Sam** Watch out, Matt. Your jacket's in the water!
**Matt** Oh, no! It's got my wallet and passport in it! It's all your fault, Gwen.
**Gwen** My fault?
**Jasmin** Look, just calm down, you two. What about using your oar, Sam? Get it before it sinks!
**Sam** I'm trying. But I can't get it.
**Gwen** Why don't you get in the water, Matt? It was your fault.
**Matt** No way!
**Jasmin** We could call the boat centre.
**Matt** Yeah, shall we do that?
**Sam** No, it's okay. Hold me, Jas, so I don't fall in.
**Jasmin** Right.
**Sam** Got it! Here it is! And your wallet and passport are fine. You're lucky, Matt.
**Matt** Thanks, Sam. Sorry about that, everyone.
**Gwen** Oh, all right. Come on, let's get back.

## Skills

## Speaking

**3** Look at the Key Expressions.

**Key Expressions: Making Suggestions**

What **about** using your oar?
Why **don't** you get in the water?
We **could** call the boat centre.
**Shall** we do that?
**Let's** get back.

**4** Work in pairs. Use the Key Expressions and make suggestions for the situations.

A *Let's have a surprise party for him.*
B *No, why don't we all go go-karting?*

1 It's your friend's birthday on Saturday and you're discussing what to do for him.
2 You are with your friend. You can hear shouts of 'Help' from next door.
3 It's late and you've both missed the last bus home.

**5** Work in pairs. Imagine you are lost in a forest. Use the ideas below, make suggestions and decide what to do.

- it's cold • it's starting to rain • it's getting dark
- you are hungry • you have a mobile phone
- there is a river • you have a tent
- you have matches • you have a compass

A *Why don't we make a fire to keep warm?*
B *No, it's raining. Everything is wet. Shall we ...?*

**6** Compare your suggestions with another pair of students.

## Everyday Listening

**1** Listen to the conversation in the travel agent's. How do the couple decide to travel? How long is their journey going to be?

**2** Listen again. Complete the travel information.

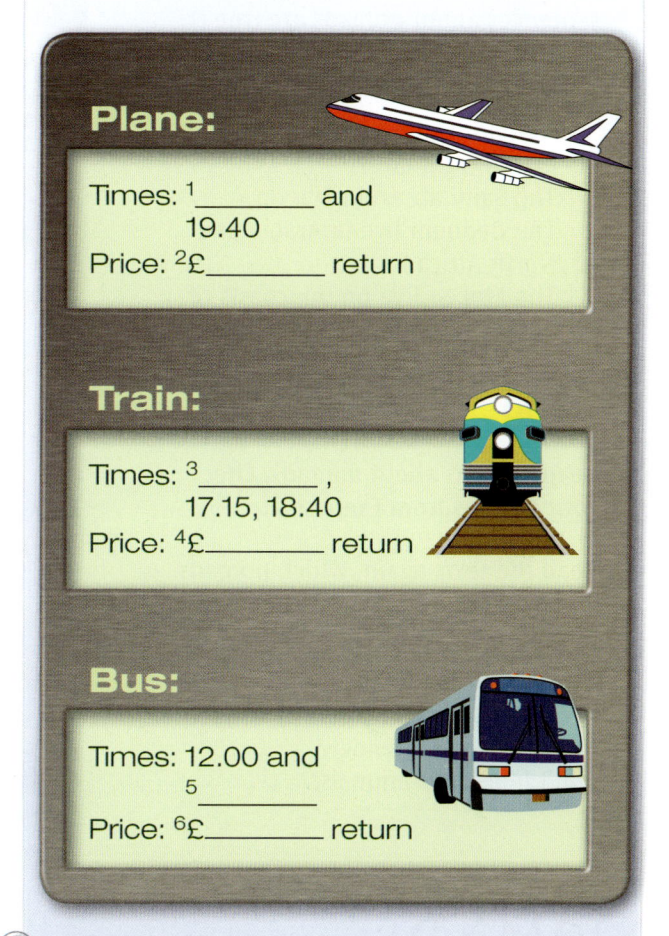

**Plane:**
Times: ¹_____ and 19.40
Price: ²£_____ return

**Train:**
Times: ³_____ , 17.15, 18.40
Price: ⁴£_____ return

**Bus:**
Times: 12.00 and ⁵_____
Price: ⁶£_____ return

**3 Pronunciation** Listen to the sound of the letter 'g' in these words. Repeat the words.

1 /g/ group
2 /dʒ/ generation
3 /ŋ/ everything

**4** Look at the words below. How do you say them? Put them in the correct group, 1, 2 or 3.

a**g**e aller**g**y an**g**ry annoyin**g** ar**g**ue
di**g**ital ener**g**etic for**g**et **g**ame
**g**raffiti **g**ymnastics livin**g** room lo**g**ical
or**g**anised ori**g**inal rin**g** shoppin**g**
teena**g**er washin**g**-up

**5** Listen and check your answers. Repeat the words.

**TIMEOUT!** ▶ Page 99, Exercise 15

55

# Across Cultures 3

## Warm-up

**1** Listen to three pieces of music. Match them with the photos (a–c).

**2** Look at the photos. Do you think the sentences about nomads are true (T) or false (F)?

1. ☐ Nomads travel for fun.
2. ☐ Nomads often live in places with extreme climates.
3. ☐ The Sami are from Siberia.
4. ☐ The Bedouin live in Arabia and North Africa.
5. ☐ The Moken live on the coasts of Thailand and Burma (Myanmar).

## Reading

**3** Read the text about nomads. Check your guesses from Exercise 2.

**4** Read the texts again. Which nomads:
1. welcome strangers?
2. travel in the summer?
3. are good at finding water?
4. live on land for only part of the year?
5. use modern technology?
6. don't look after animals?

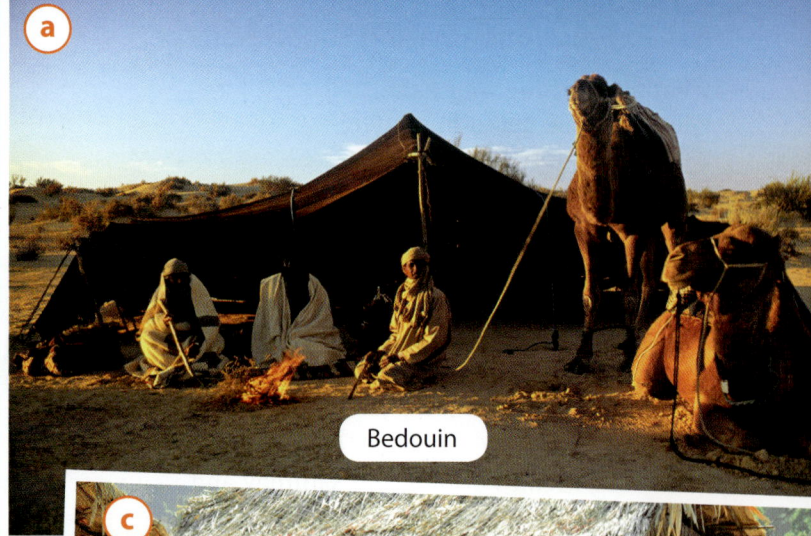

a — Bedouin
c — Moken

# NOMADS

For nomads, being on the move is part of everyday life. Some move to look for food for their animals or themselves, others travel to buy and sell things. Actually, there are not many nomads left in the world nowadays but some nomadic people still survive.

## The Reindeer People

The Sami live in northern Scandinavia. Most of them now have 'normal' jobs in towns and cities but some carry on their traditional way of life. In early summer, they go on a long journey north with their reindeers. The Sami take them far into the Arctic Circle to find grass and plants to eat. When autumn begins, they take the reindeers south again. Nowadays, the Sami use snowmobiles and mobile phones when they are looking after their animals. However, they still wear their colourful costumes and sing their traditional songs.

## Desert Survivors

The word 'Bedouin' means 'desert inhabitant'. Many Bedouins live in towns in Arabia and North Africa but some still make trips into the desert to get food for their camels. The camels, or 'ships of the desert', carry everything and provide food (milk and meat) and shelter (wool for tents). Bedouin hospitality is famous: they give strangers food and water. Bedouins know many tricks to find water. For example, when they see insects or birds, they know water is usually near.

## Sea Gypsies

The Moken are often called 'sea gypsies'. Some follow their traditional lifestyle in the coastal areas of Thailand and Myanmar. During the rainy season, when the sea is rough, they live in huts on the beach but for the rest of the year they live on their boats. They catch seafood and sell it in fishing villages. Moken children learn to swim before they can walk. They can see underwater twice as clearly as the rest of us and can stay underwater twice as long! The Moken people know the sea very well – before the tsunami in 2005, they left the sea and looked for high ground.

Sami

**8 Word Quiz** Complete the sentences with the words in brackets.
1 They wanted to _____ a bank and _____ a million pounds. (*steal/rob*)
2 I _____ a lot of money but I still try to _____ the lottery. (*earn/win*)
3 _____ this cup to the kitchen, please. And can you _____ me a biscuit? (*bring/take*)

▶ Word Bank, page 107

## Speaking

**9** Work in pairs. Ask and answer the questions.
1 Have you ever moved house? How old were you? How did you feel?
2 Would you like to move to another place? Where would you like to live?
3 Would you like to live like a nomad? Why/Why not?

**5** What do the blue words in the text refer to?

*1 some — nomads*

1 some (line 2)     5 them (line 11)
2 others (line 3)   6 some (line 20)
3 some (line 9)     7 it (line 31)
4 they (line 10)    8 they (line 33)

**6** Look at the Word Builder. The words in **bold** are often confusing. What are they in your language?

### Word Builder

**Actually**, there are not many nomads left in the world **nowadays**.

Some still go on **journeys** across the desert.
They still make **trips** into the desert.

They **carry** their things.
They still **wear** their colourful costumes.

**7** Choose the correct word.
1 Are you from England? No, I'm from Scotland, *actually / nowadays*.
2 Traffic pollution wasn't a problem a hundred years ago but it is *actually / nowadays*.
3 The train *journey / trip* took four hours.
4 My dad went on a business *journey / trip* to London.
5 She's *carrying / wearing* a lovely dress.
6 The camels *carry / wear* huge baskets.

## PROJECT

### Touring your country

1 Choose interesting places. Write notes about the places to visit and things to do.
2 Use your notes to write a description of the tour.
3 Copy a map and draw the route on it.
4 Find pictures to add to your description.
5 Make a wall poster with your description, maps and pictures, like the one below.

**Days 1 and 2:** Arrive in Edinburgh. There are many things to see, like Edinburgh Castle and Holyrood Palace. Visit the National Gallery to see some great paintings or go shopping for souvenirs on the Royal Mile.

**Day 3:** Visit the beautiful university city of St Andrews, the home of golf. St Andrews has got a good beach but the water is freezing!

**Day 4:** Travel north to Inverness to see the monster in Loch Ness. Then …

# Study Corner 5

## Language Check

**1** What are the types of transport?

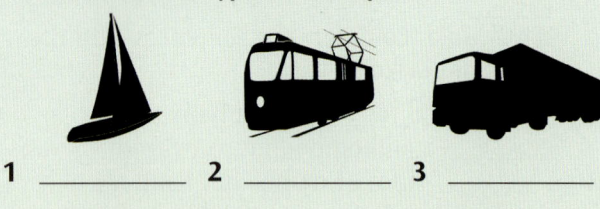

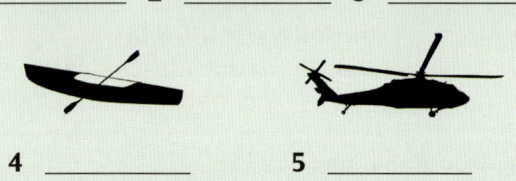

1 _____  2 _____  3 _____
4 _____  5 _____

**2** Complete the gaps with the names of jobs.

6  A _____ grows food or looks after animals.
7  A _____ takes photos.
8  A _____ catches criminals or directs traffic.
9  A _____ usually does paperwork and answers the phone in an office.
10 A _____ talks to the camera and gives information.

**3** Complete the compound words in the sentences.

11 Rare mountain gorillas live in the **rain** _____ in Uganda.
12 Australia and New Zealand are **English-** _____ countries.
13 My dad's hobby is **bird** _____ .
14 We stayed in a **five-** _____ hotel.
15 There are fifteen **national** _____ in Britain.

Vocabulary ☐ / 15

**4** Put the verbs in brackets in the Past Simple or Present Perfect.

16 _____ you _____ the teacher your homework yet? (give)
England 17 _____ the World Cup once.
They 18 _____ it in London in 1966. (win)
I 19 _____ in Paris last year on holiday.
I 20 _____ there twice. (be)

**5** Complete the gaps with one word.

A Have you 21 _____ been to Italy?
B Yes, but I've 22 _____ visited Rome.
A Has your sister finished her maths homework 23 _____ ?
B Yes, she's 24 _____ done it but she hasn't finished her science 25 _____ .

Grammar ☐ / 10

**6** Complete the gaps with one word.

A It's Amber's birthday tomorrow.
B 26 _____ we get her a present?
A Good idea! What 27 _____ getting her a CD?
B No, she downloads all her music. We 28 _____ get her a T-shirt.
A Okay. 29 _____ go to Shirtz Shop.
B 30 _____ don't we look in the market first? It's cheaper.
A Yeah, that's a great idea.

Key Expressions ☐ / 5

## Feedback

- Listen and check your answers to the Language Check. Write down your scores.
- Look at the table below. Check where you made mistakes.

| Wrong answers: | Look again at: |
| --- | --- |
| Numbers 1–5 | Get Ready – Key Words |
| Numbers 6–10 | Unit 13 – Key Words |
| Numbers 11–15 | Unit 14 – Word Builder |
| Numbers 16–25 | Unit 13 – Grammar |
| Numbers 26–30 | Unit 15 – Key Expressions |

- Now do the exercises in Language Check 5 of the Workbook.

## Study Help: Explaining words

When you don't know a word, try to describe it.

*We stayed in a sort of hotel for young people. (youth hostel)*
*It's a kind of black and white bear and it lives in China. (panda)*

- What are these words?
1 It's a kind of small boat for one or two people.
2 He/She is a sort of waiter/waitress. He/She brings the food on aeroplanes.
3 It's a kind of car. It's good for safaris.

- Work in pairs. Each choose three words from this module. Describe them to your partner using *sort of* or *kind of*. Your partner guesses the word.

A *It's a sort of expensive hotel.*
B *A five-star hotel?*
A *Yes!*

## Module 6

- Talk about films and books; give instructions.
- Read about films and books.
- Listen to a scene from a film.
- Write a short film review.
- Learn about future predictions; Present Perfect and Past Simple.

a) Nanny McPhee
b) The Spy Who Came in from the Cold
c) The Other Boleyn Girl
d) The Bourne Identity

# Films and Books

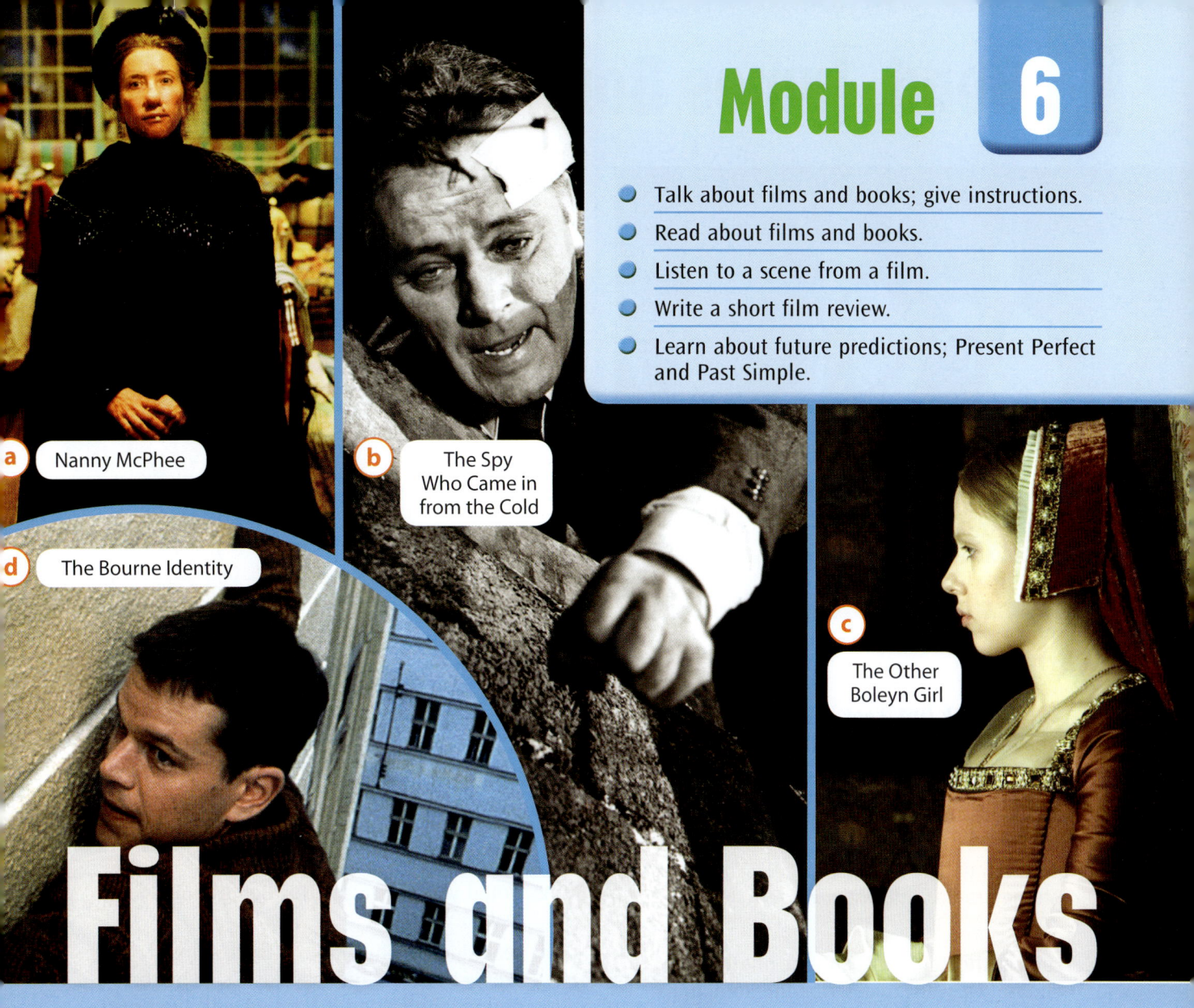

## Get Ready

**1** Look at the Key Words and the photos (a–d). What kinds of films are they? Which of the films are also books?

a) children's

**Key Words: Films and Books**

Adjectives: adventure   children's   crime   fantasy   historical   horror   science fiction   spy   war
Nouns: thriller

**2** Listen to three people talking about the books and films in the photos. Check your guesses from Exercise 1.

**3** Listen again. Are the sentences true (T) or false (F)?

1. ☐ Speaker 1 liked the film more than the book.
2. ☐ Speaker 2 and his sister think the book is better than the film.
3. ☐ Speaker 3 liked the film more than the book.

**4** Speak Out  Work in pairs. Ask and answer the questions below. Tell the class.

1. What books have you read recently?
2. What films have you seen recently?
3. Have you seen any films of books or read any books of films? Did you think the film or the book was better?

**5** Game  Work in pairs.

- You have three minutes! Think of a film for each category in the Key Words.
- Compare your list with another pair and calculate your score.

**Score:**
Ten points for a film title in English.
Five points for a film in your language.
Two points if both pairs have the same film.

Team A   *Historical film – The King's Speech.*
Team B   *For us, Gladiator. That's ten points each. Now our turn.*

59

# 16 Bond, James Bond

From Russia With Love, 1963

For Your Eyes Only, 1981

## Warm-up

**1** 🔊 **Speak Out** Look at the Key Words. What kinds of films do you like? Tell the class.

**Key Words: Films**
Adjectives: action   romantic
Nouns: animation   comedy
costume drama   musical   western

**2** Look at the Key Words and the photos. Choose *one* word to describe the Bond films.

**3** Find three more words in the Key Words on page 59 that describe the Bond films.

**4** Read the text about 007 and look at the photos. Answer the questions.

1 Where is Bond from?
2 Who created the character of Bond?
3 What shows that Bond is a popular character?

## Reading and Listening

**5** Read and listen to the dialogue. Who knows more about James Bond, Tom or Ann?

**Ann** Would you like to see this Bond film? It looks really exciting!

**Tom** Yeah, look at this photo – there's fire everywhere, the military base is going to explode. And Bond is fighting with the driver – they're going to crash!

**Ann** There are enemy soldiers everywhere and he's alone. They're going to kill him!

**Tom** Kill Bond?! That'll never happen!

**6** Read the text about Bond films. Do you agree? Why/Why not?

### 007 Factfile

James Bond, or 007, a British spy, was created by the writer, Ian Fleming. Twenty-three James Bond films have been made so far. The first one, *Dr No*, was made in 1962 and starred Sean Connery. The last one, *Quantum of Solace* with Daniel Craig, was made in 2008. Six actors have played Bond so far. The most famous are Sean Connery, Pierce Brosnan and Daniel Craig.
The Bond films always have great title songs and they have been sung by some of the world's most famous singers. For example, Paul McCartney sang *Live and Let Die* and *Die Another Day* was sung by Madonna.

### Will Bond Ever Die?

Will 007 ever disappear from the cinema screen? It seems unlikely. Over two billion people have seen a Bond film. People will always enjoy watching action films so new Bond films will always be made. However, they may be less popular with younger audiences because they prefer 3D films like *Avatar*, packed with computer-generated special effects. In the past, Bond films have won awards for special effects but they probably won't win any more. I predict that, in the future, they might have *less* technology because a typical Bond fan is more interested in the plot and the characters. The films will certainly win some more Oscars but the ones for special effects will probably go to science fiction or fantasy films like *Inception*.

Joanna Grant
film critic

# Grammar

*Quantum of Solace, 2008*

## Grammar: Predictions

**7** Look at the predictions from Exercises 5 and 6. Underline the verb forms referring to the future.

1. The military base is going to explode.
2. They probably won't win any more.
3. The films will certainly win some more Oscars.
4. They might have less technology.
5. They may be less popular with younger audiences.

**8** Complete the rules (1–3) with verb forms (a–c).

a) *be going to* + infinitive
b) *will/won't* + infinitive
c) *may/might* + infinitive

1. We use _____ to express our opinions and beliefs about the future (often with *I think, I hope, certainly/maybe/probably/perhaps*).
2. We use _____ to express predictions based on evidence in the present situation.
3. We use _____ to express an uncertain prediction or guess about the future.

## Practice

**9** Complete the predictions with *will, won't, may/might*.

1. Daniel Craig __will__ probably star in the next Bond film.
2. Bond _____ certainly never get married.
3. I'm sure Bond _____ die.
4. Lady Gaga _____ sing the next Bond theme song.
5. Bond's next enemy _____ be an alien.

**10** Complete the predictions with the correct form of *be going to*.

1. The sky is dark and the wind is getting stronger. There __'s going to be__ a storm. (be)
2. The engines have stopped, the plane _____ ! (crash)
3. Can you see the shark? It _____ the swimmer! (attack)
4. There are crowds of people queuing for tickets. The cinema _____ (be) full.

**11** Look at the picture and the words in the box. Make predictions using *be going to, will/won't* and *may/might*.

| fall into the sea   die   use a parachute |
| kiss   save the girl   escape             |

*They're going to fall into the sea.*

## Your Turn

**12** Work in pairs. Think of a TV series you both watch and predict what will happen in the next episode.

A *I think Sheila will fall in love with Derek.*
B *That's impossible. She's in love with Tom.*

**13** **Speak Out** Tell the class your predictions. Don't say the title of the series. The class guess the title.

TIMEOUT! ▶ Page 100, Exercise 16

# 17 Classics

## Warm-up

**1** Look at the Key Words. Which types of books do you like reading? Which reference books have you used? What is your favourite format for reading?

**Key Words:** Books and Reading

**Literature:** fiction e.g. graphic novel   novel   play
short story   poetry   non-fiction e.g. biography   history
**Reference:** address book   atlas   dictionary
encyclopedia   instruction manual   phone book
**Format:** CD-Rom   comic   e-book   hardback
online e.g. blog   paperback

**3** Look at the Reading Help.

**Reading Help: Difficult words and phrases**
- Underline words or groups of words you don't know.
- Read the sentences before and after and try to guess the meaning of the underlined words from the context.
- Write new words and expressions in your vocabulary book.

## Reading

**2** Read the text. Which books (1–3) do the pictures (a–c) illustrate?

**1**
J.D. Salinger's only novel, *The Catcher in the Rye*, was published in 1951. It tells the story of sixteen-year-old Holden Caulfield who fails his exams and runs away from school. He spends three days in New York where he comes across different people and situations that make him think about life. The book received mixed reactions: it was required reading in some schools, although it didn't get past the censors in others. Many film studios wanted to make a film of the book. However, Salinger always refused.

Salinger was a very private man. His last official photograph was taken in 1953 and he gave his last interview in 1980.

**2**
Ursula Le Guin's fantasy novel, *A Wizard of Earthsea*, is the first of the three Earthsea books. It is a classic battle between good and evil. It is the story of a clever young wizard, Sparrowhawk, who releases a terrible monster into the world. At first he tries to get away from the monster but in the end he learns that he must face his fear.

Some people say that the Harry Potter books are similar to the Earthsea trilogy. Although many critics think that the Earthsea books are better than the Harry Potter books, they are not as well-known.

**3**
Harper Lee's classic novel, *To Kill a Mockingbird*, was published in 1960. It is the story of Scout Finch and her brother Jem growing up in 1930s Alabama. In the two years that the book covers, the children find out a lot about the prejudices of their neighbours when their father, a lawyer, defends a black man in court. Although the man is innocent, he is sent to prison because of his race. Eventually, he tries to escape from prison and he is killed.

*To Kill a Mockingbird* is an incredibly successful book: millions of people have read it and it was made into a film. However, Harper Lee never published another novel.

**4** Find the underlined words and expressions in the text and match them with the meanings (1–6). Use the advice in the Reading Help.

1 someone who checks books, films etc. to make sure they aren't dangerous
2 someone whose job is to give their opinion of books, films etc.
3 to escape from a person or place
4 to let something go free
5 when people don't like/trust someone because they are different
6 to deal with a difficult problem

**5** The verbs in the Word Builder are in red in the text. Find them and guess their meaning.

### Word Builder

**come across** a person or thing
**get past** somebody or something
**get away from** a person or place
**find out** some information

**6** Complete the sentences with verbs from the Word Builder in the correct form.

1 I was surprised the violent scenes in the film _____ the censors.
2 When my dad wants to _____ us, he goes and reads a book.
3 We had to _____ about Alabama and Mississippi for our geography homework.
4 While I was looking for something to read, I _____ my mum's school copy of *The Catcher in the Rye*.

▶ Word Bank, page 106

**7** Look at the Sentence Builder. Find more examples of the linking words in the text.

### Sentence Builder

**Although** the man is innocent, he is sent to prison because of his race.

It was required reading in some schools, **although** it didn't get past the censors in others.

Many film studios wanted to make a film of the book. **However**, Salinger always refused.

―**Fact or Fiction?**―
The film director, Steven Spielberg, appears somewhere in all of his films.
Answer on page 92.

# Skills

**8** Rewrite the sentences in two ways using *although* and *however*.

1 Very few people knew what J.D. Salinger looked like. He was very famous.
2 *The Catcher in the Rye* is an old book. I really like it.
3 She loved the Earthsea books. She hasn't read other books by Ursula Le Guin.
4 He hasn't read *To Kill a Mockingbird*. He's seen the film.
5 Harper Lee was a very talented writer. She never wrote another novel.

## Speaking

**9** Work in pairs and do the book quiz. Then think of two book questions to ask the class.

### FILM AND BOOK QUIZ

1 Who wrote *Frankenstein*?
   a) Jane Austen   b) Anne Brontë
   c) Mary Shelley

2 Which two authors are from Latin America?
   a) Miguel de Cervantes   b) Vargas Llosa
   c) Isabel Allende

3 What kind of fiction *didn't* Shakespeare write?
   a) poems   b) novels   c) plays

4 When did J.K. Rowling publish the first Harry Potter book?
   a) 1986   b) 1997   c) 2004

5 Which author is famous for writing fantasy novels?
   a) Stephenie Meyer   b) Agatha Christie
   c) Sara Paretsky

6 Which Czech writer became the country's president?
   a) Franz Kafka   b) Milan Kundera
   c) Vaclav Havel

7 Which character from a novel has been in the most films?
   a) Don Quixote   b) Dracula
   c) Sherlock Holmes

8 What have Orhan Pamuk, Herta Müller and Imre Kertész all won?
   a) the Oscar for best film script
   b) the Nobel Prize for Literature
   c) the Golden Dagger prize for crime writing

Check your answers on page 91.

**TIMEOUT!** ▶ Page 100, Exercise 17

# 18 The Long Goodbye

## Warm-up

1 Look at the photo. What is happening in it? What kind of scene are they filming?

## Reading and Listening

2 Read and listen to the dialogue. Check your guesses from Exercise 1.

*The group film a 'romantic' scene from the 1890s.*

**Gwen** Action!
**Matt** So, goodbye my love.
**Jasmin** Darling, will you write to me every day? I'm going to be so lonely.
**Matt** But I'll be in the jungle, Arabella.
**Jasmin** You just don't love me, Hector!
**Gwen** Cut! We need more feeling. Jasmin, move closer to the train so Matt can take your hand.
**Matt** I can't reach her from the window.
**Gwen** Okay, Matt, go and stand on the platform. Stand near the door so you can jump on the train when it's leaving.
**Matt** Hey, I'm not a stuntman!
**Gwen** Don't worry, Matt. Jas, don't stand there because your back's to the camera.
**Jasmin** Sorry! I don't know where to stand.
**Gwen** Move over there and face Matt. That's right. Now Sam, move the camera over here to get a better shot.
**Sam** Okay.
**Gwen** Jas, stand a bit closer to Matt so that you can kiss him when he leaves. Remember, you're in love!
**Matt** I'm not sure when to get on the train.
**Gwen** When the train moves, jump on it and wave to Jas.
**Sam** That's going to be hard to film.
**Matt** And dangerous.
**Gwen** Look, it'll be fine. Let's have a break.

**Skills**

**3** Are the sentences true (T), false (F) or is there no information (NI)?
1. ☐ Jasmin's character gets angry.
2. ☐ Matt's character is going to India.
3. ☐ Matt doesn't want to jump on the train.
4. ☐ Gwen is very confident.
5. ☐ Sam has never used the camera before.

**4** Look at the Sentence Builder.

> **Sentence Builder**
> I don't know **where to** stand.
> I'm not sure **when to** get on the train.

**5** Complete the sentences with the words in the box.

> how   what   when   where   who

1. I don't know _____ to wear for the party.
2. We don't know _____ to ask about the homework.
3. They don't know _____ to sit.
4. Do you know _____ to do this maths homework?
5. I'm not sure _____ to leave the house. Is six o'clock too early?

## Speaking

**6** Complete the Key Expressions from the text.

> **Key Expressions:**
> Instructions and Reasons
> 1. Jasmin, move closer to the train _____ Matt can take your hand.
> 2. Don't stand there _____ your back's to the camera.
> 3. Move the camera over here _____ get a better shot.
> 4. Stand a bit closer to Matt _____ that you can kiss him.

**7 Game** Imagine you are a film director. Think of reasons for these instructions.
1. Stand behind the door so …
2. Go outside to …
3. Don't open the box because …
4. Get in the car so that …
5. Turn on the radio to …

**8** Work in pairs. Take turns to give your partner instructions.

Director: *Stand behind the door.*
Actor:    *Why?*

## Everyday Listening 🔊

**1** Guess the answers to these questions about the final version of the film scene.

1. What is Hector going to look for in Africa?
   a) a lost city   b) an explorer
   c) his father
2. What is Arabella going to have?
   a) a problem   b) an illness
   c) a baby
3. What is Hector's reaction to the news?
   a) he is angry   b) he is happy
   c) he is sad
4. Who can go instead?
   a) Hector's friend   b) Hector's brother
   c) Hector's boss
5. What does Hector decide to do?
   a) leave for Africa   b) stay with Arabella
   c) get a later train

**3.25 2** Listen and check your guesses from Exercise 1.

**3.26 3** Listen again. Evaluate these things (1 – very bad, 5 – fantastic).
- Matt's acting ☐   • Jasmin's acting ☐
- the story ☐   • the sound effects ☐

**3.27 4 Listen closely** Listen and complete the expressions.
1. _____ _____ fair.
2. _____ life.
3. _____ _____ sorry.
4. _____ _____ all right.
5. _____ _____ it?
6. _____ _____ sure.
7. _____ _____ _____ it!
8. _____ wonderful!

**TIMEOUT!** ▶ Page 101, Exercise 18

## Your Challenge

### Film Review

**1** *Avatar* (2009), directed by *Titanic* director James Cameron, is a special-effects-packed science-fiction film. The stars are Sam Worthington, Zoe Saldana and Sigourney Weaver.

**2** *Avatar* takes place in 2154 when the world is dying. Humans travel to a distant planet called Pandora to find a valuable material which will save Earth. There they meet the Na'vi, blue-skinned, athletic aliens who haven't destroyed their planet. The humans make an avatar – half human, half Na'vi – to get information about Pandora. The character Jake Scully is chosen for this job. However, he falls in love with an alien, Neytiri, and decides to join the Na'vi.

**3** Although this film is 163 minutes long, it never gets boring because the special effects are extraordinary. It's one of the most expensive films ever made and the use of CGI plus 3D is brilliant. However, the characters aren't always convincing and some of the script is unnatural as well. Also, I found the environmental message annoying.

**4** I don't usually enjoy films like *Star Wars* and *The Matrix* but I really enjoyed *Avatar*. It's worth seeing it for the special effects. Don't miss it!

### Writing: Film review

1. Look at the photo. Have you seen the film? What did you think of it?

2. Read the review of *Avatar*. Is it generally positive or negative?

### Text Builder

3. Match the paragraphs (1–4) with the topics (a–d).
   a) recommendations   c) opinions
   b) background to the story   d) basic information

4. Look at the linking words in blue in the text. Which do we use for:
   • addition?   • contrast?   • examples?

5. Write a review of a film you have seen recently.

**STEP 1** Write notes about the film.
- basic information: *title, date, kind of film, director, stars*
- background to the story: *where? / when? / what happens?*
- opinions: *acting / story / special effects and photography, music*
- recommendations: *it's (not) worth seeing, I (don't) recommend it*

**STEP 2** Use your notes to write the review. Write four short paragraphs.

**STEP 3** Check spelling, vocabulary and grammar.

**STEP 4** Work in groups. Read each other's reviews. Do you agree with them?

*I don't agree with Anna's review. I thought the film was brilliant.*

# Understanding Grammar: Present Perfect and Past Simple

**1** Read the text about Jodie Foster and look at the photos. Have you seen the films? What did you think of them?

### BIODATA

Jodie Foster, an American actress and film director, was born in 1962. She has appeared in over 100 films. She started her film career as a child. In 1976, she appeared in *Taxi Driver* with Robert De Niro and was nominated for an Oscar. In 1985, she graduated from Yale University with a degree in literature. So far, she has won two Oscars for Best Actress. She won her first Oscar in 1988 and her second in 1991 for *The Silence of the Lambs*. Recently, she has directed and produced a number of films, too.

**2** Read the text again and <u>underline</u> the verbs in the Past Simple and the Present Perfect.

**3** Look at the verbs you <u>underlined</u> in Exercise 1. Match the tenses (1–2) with the uses and timelines (a–b).

1 Present Perfect    2 Past Simple

a) we know exactly when the event happened and we don't want to link it with the present

now

b) the event happened in the period of time before now and has influence on the present situation

now

**4** Read the sentences and translate the verbs in **bold** into your language. Is the translation the same or different?
1 She **has appeared** in over 100 films.
2 In 1976, she **appeared** in *Taxi Driver*.

**5** Match the sentences (1–2) with the people (a–b).

| 1 He's got two Oscars. | a) a dead actor |
| 2 He got two Oscars.   | b) a living actor |
| 1 She's become famous. | a) a new star |
| 2 She became famous.   | b) an old star |

**6** Put the verbs in brackets in the Present Perfect or Past Simple.
1 Hollywood _____ (produce) many superstars.
2 _____ (you, watch) the Oscar awards ceremony on TV last night?
3 Tom Cruise _____ (receive) three Oscar nominations but he _____ (not win) an Oscar.
4 Leonardo DiCaprio _____ (act) in over twenty films.
5 Alfred Hitchcock _____ (not like) dark-haired actresses.

**7** Read the dialogue. What tense is used to start the conversation? What tense is used to ask about details?

**Tom** Have you seen any good films lately?
**Mike** Yes, I have. I watched *Jaws* last night.
**Tom** Where did you watch it?
**Mike** At home. My dad's got it on DVD.
**Tom** Did you like it?
**Mike** Yes. It's old and the special effects are a bit funny but I was scared anyway.

**8** Work in pairs. Use the cues to talk about your experiences.

A *Have you been to the United States?*
B *Yes, I have.*
A *Did you go to Hollywood?*
B *No, I didn't.*

1 be to the United States / go to Hollywood
2 talk to an actor / who
3 act in a play / what role
4 write a film review / what film
5 see a *Star Wars* film / like the special effects
6 watch a horror film / be scared

67

# Study Corner 6

## Language Check

**1 Complete the words in the sentences.**

1 The original *Star Wars* films were great s _ _ _ _ _ _ _ f _ _ _ _ _ _ _ films.
2 *Toy Story* and *Shrek* are great a _ _ _ _ _ _ _ _ _ films.
3 I love h _ _ _ _ _ stories like *Dracula* and *Frankenstein*.
4 *The Lord of the Rings* is the best f _ _ _ _ _ _ novel I've ever read.
5 Although the Cold War is over, people still love s _ _ films and novels.
6 The t _ _ _ _ _ _ _ was very exciting and I couldn't stop reading it.

**2 Complete the gaps with the words in the box.**

| across   out   past   from |
|---|

7 Did you ever find _____ the author's name?
8 I came _____ an old friend in the bookshop.
9 He got _____ the defender and scored a goal.
10 She ran quickly and got away _____ the dog.

Vocabulary ☐ / 10

**3 Put the verbs in brackets in the Past Simple or Present Perfect.**

Nearly all of Steven Spielberg's films [11]_____ (be) very popular. He [12]_____ (direct) many box-office hits like *Jaws* and *Jurassic Park*. He [13]_____ (make) his biggest commercial hit, *E.T. the Extra-Terrestrial*, in 1982. So far in his career, he [14]_____ (win) two Oscars for Best Director. He [15]_____ (win) his first in 1993 (*Schindler's List*) and his second in 1998 (*Saving Private Ryan*).

**4 Choose the correct word.**

16 Next year we *may / won't* read 'Hamlet' in English or maybe 'Romeo and Juliet'.
17 He *might / will* win an Oscar but I don't think so.
18 We *might / will* study 'Of Mice and Men' next term – it's one of our exams titles.
19 Special effects *may / will* certainly get better.
20 I don't think she *might / will* win a prize for her poetry.
21 I'm sure e-books *may / will* replace paperbacks in the next twenty years.
22 They *might / won't* make another 'Lord of the Rings' film because there are only three books.
23 The producers haven't decided yet but they *may / will* make another Bourne film.
24 He *might / won't* get the part – he isn't tall enough.
25 They probably *might / will* invent something better than DVDs.

Grammar ☐ / 15

**5 Complete the instructions with *because*, *so* or *to*.**

Keep a vocabulary book [26]_____ put new words in. Have a section for expressions [27]_____ they are very important to learn. Write an example sentence and a translation in your own language [28]_____ that you can use your vocabulary book for revision. Use different colours [29]_____ help you organise your book (e.g. different colours for nouns, verbs and adjectives). Mark the main stress [30]_____ you don't forget it.

Key Expressions ☐ / 5

## Feedback

- Listen and check your answers to the Language Check. Write down your scores.
- Look at the table below. Check where you made mistakes.

| Wrong answers: | Look again at: |
|---|---|
| Numbers 1–6 | Get Ready – Key Words |
| Numbers 7–10 | Unit 17 – Word Builder |
| Numbers 11–15 | Understanding Grammar |
| Numbers 16–25 | Unit 16 – Grammar |
| Numbers 26–30 | Unit 18 – Key Expressions |

- Now do the exercises in Language Check 6 of the Workbook.

## Study Help: Multi-part verbs

Write new multi-part verbs (e.g. take part in, pick up) in your vocabulary notebook.

Write a translation in your language.

Write a sentence with an example of the verb.

*come round*
*Two friends came round to my house last night.*

- Put the multi-part verbs from this module in your book. Follow the above advice.

# Module 7

- Talk about music and give a presentation.
- Read about music and musical instruments.
- Listen to a conversation about a music event.
- Write a short biography.
- Learn about relative clauses.

# Music

## Get Ready

**1** Look at the Key Words. Can you add any styles of music?

> **Key Words:** Music
>
> **Styles:** classical  dance  grunge  heavy metal  hip hop  jazz  pop  punk  rap  rock
> **Adjectives:** aggressive  catchy  fast  happy  heavy  jazzy  lively  loud  monotonous  relaxing  repetitive  romantic  sad  slow

**2** Listen to six extracts. Identify the style of music and choose adjectives to describe it.

*1  pop music – catchy and repetitive*

**3** Listen to three people (a–c). Complete the table with styles from the Key Words and these musicians and singers.

1 Beethoven   4 Eminem      7 Kings of Leon
2 Beyoncé     5 Green Day   8 Snoop Dogg
3 Coldplay    6 Katy Perry  9 The Saturdays

|   | Favourite styles | Doesn't like | Favourite singers/musicians |
|---|---|---|---|
| a |   |   | 1 / 4 / 8 |
| b |   |   |   |
| c |   |   |   |

**4** Work in groups and prepare questions for a music survey about:

- styles • singers • groups.

**5** Ask and answer your questions and complete a table like the one in Exercise 3.

A *What style of music do you like?*
B *I like hip hop and rap and some kinds of rock.*

**6** **Speak Out** Tell the class the results of your survey.

*Three of us like rap and one doesn't. All of us like ...*

# 19 Sixty Years of Pop

## Warm-up

**1** Work in pairs. Match the photos (1–5) with the music styles (a–e).

a) girl band pop   c) reggae   e) Tamla Motown
b) New Romantic   d) Rock 'n' Roll

## Reading

**2** Read the text and check your guesses from Exercise 1. Which important events and people do you think are missing from the text?

## Grammar: Defining relative clauses

**3** Look at the sentences (1–2) from the text. What information (a, b or c) do the underlined relative clauses add to the sentences?

a) tell us when or where something happened
b) describe or tell us about a person or thing
c) say what happened

> 1  He recorded a single.
>    He recorded a single <u>which changed the world of popular music for ever</u>. ____
> 2  The stars include Stevie Wonder.
>    The stars <u>whose careers started at the Hit Factory</u> include Stevie Wonder. ____

# The History of Pop

It's about sixty years since parents first said, 'Turn it down.' What has happened in those sixty years?

### The '50s
In 1954, nineteen-year-old Elvis Presley walked into Sun Studios in Memphis, in the United States. He recorded a single which changed the world of popular music forever. It was called *That's All Right Mamma*. Very quickly, Elvis went from being an unknown truck driver to the King of Rock 'n' Roll. His performances shocked parents but young people loved him.

### The '60s
Detroit in the United States is the city where Tamla Motown was born and it is the music that defined the '60s. Berry Gordy is the record producer that started the Tamla Motown recording studio. It was called the Hit Factory because they made so many number one hits there. The stars whose careers started at the Hit Factory include Stevie Wonder, Smokie Robinson and Diana Ross.

### The '70s
1975 is the year when the whole world learnt about reggae. *No Woman, No Cry* by Bob Marley and the Wailers is the single that made Jamaican reggae internationally popular. It was Bob Marley's success that opened the door for other reggae musicians.

### The '80s
Pop videos became as important as the music when MTV started in 1981. Bands like Duran Duran and Spandau Ballet used videos to advertise their songs. These bands were New Romantics whose songs about love and dancing were a reaction to punk rock. Their clothes were very different, too: they wore designer clothes, eye make-up and had blond streaks in their hair.

### The '90s
The first all-girl band started in 1994 when a manager advertised for girls who could sing and dance. The five he chose became the Spice Girls who were very popular with young girls. The girl group became symbols of 'Cool Britannia' and they had a lot of hit records before they stopped recording together in 2000.

### The '00s
Technology has completely changed the way people buy and listen to music. In 2000, nineteen-year-old Shawn Fanning launched Napster so people could download music from the Internet. MP3 players meant music was digital so people could buy single tracks. Musicians used the Internet to communicate directly with their fans.

## Grammar

**4** Read the phrases (1–7) from the text and complete the rules (a–e) with the relative pronouns *who*, *which*, *that*, *whose*, *when* and *where*.

1 a single **which** changed the world of popular music
2 the city **where** Tamla Motown was born
3 the record producer **that** started the Tamla Motown recording studio
4 stars **whose** careers started at the Hit Factory include Stevie Wonder
5 the single **that** made Jamaican reggae internationally popular
6 videos became as important as the music **when** MTV started
7 the Spice Girls **who** were very popular with young girls

In relative clauses we use:
a) _____ and _____ to talk about people
b) _____ and _____ to talk about things
c) _____ to talk about places
d) _____ to talk about possession
e) _____ to talk about time

**5** Compare the relative clauses (1–3). Complete the rule.

1 a group **which/that** young girls liked
2 a group young girls liked
3 a DJ **who/that** worked at the Hacienda

We can omit the relative pronoun *who*, *which* or *that* when it comes before
a) a verb
b) a noun or pronoun.

## Practice

**6** Underline the relative clauses and circle the relative pronouns in the sentences. In which sentences can you omit the relative pronouns?

1 Memphis is the place **where** Elvis Presley made his first record.
2 Diana Ross is a singer who Berry Gordy discovered.
3 I love reggae that was recorded in the 1970s.
4 Reggae is the music that Bob Marley made popular.
5 The 1950s is the time when pop was born.
6 The New Romantics are the bands who wore designer clothes.

**7** Write relative pronouns in the gaps. Put a – when the pronoun is not necessary.

A boy band is a pop group ¹ *whose* members are young male singers and dancers. Boy bands are often put together by managers or producers ² _____ select good-looking boys with dancing and singing skills. The 1990s was the period ³ _____ most boy bands were created. An important thing is the group's image ⁴ _____ is created and controlled by their managers. They decide about the clothes ⁵ _____ the group wears and promotional materials ⁶ _____ are published in teen magazines. Each member of the group is given a role ⁷ _____ they have to perform, such as 'the bad boy', or 'the nice boy'.

**8** Use the cues (1–6) to write questions for a pop quiz. Answer the questions.

1 name / actor / starred in *Walk the Line*, a film about the singer Johnny Cash?
*What is the name of the actor who starred in 'Walk the Line', a film about the singer Johnny Cash?*
2 name / female singer / sold more records than any other woman?
3 boy band / recorded *Lines, Vines and Trying Times* in 2009?
4 name / islands / reggae, ska and calypso music come from?
5 title / the album / is the biggest seller of all time?
6 name / singer / song *Poker Face* was a hit?

**9** Work in pairs. Ask and answer the questions. Check your answers on page 91.

## Your Turn

**10** Work in pairs. Use the relative pronouns in the box to make more questions about pop.

*What is the name of the group that sang 'Let It Be'?*

| that | which | who | where | when | whose |

**11** Work with another pair. Ask and answer your questions.

TIMEOUT! ▶ Page 102, Exercise 19

## 20 Music Makers

### Warm-up

1 Look at the Key Words. Which instruments can you play?

**Key Words:** Instruments

**Wind:** clarinet   flute   saxophone   trumpet
**Percussion:** drums
**String:** cello   double bass   guitar   violin
**Keyboard:** organ   piano
**Electronic:** synthesizer

2 Look at the Key Words. Listen and identify the instruments you hear.

### Reading

3 Look at the photos. What is unusual about the instruments?

4 Read the text and check your answers from Exercise 3.

The Vienna Vegetable Orchestra is a group of musicians who play vegetables. On the day of a concert, the orchestra buys fresh vegetables an hour before the performance to make their instruments. These include wind instruments made from carrots and percussion instruments made from aubergines. The sounds are amplified with microphones. The orchestra plays different musical styles from experimental electronic music to jazz. Their music is constantly developing and when they go on tour, they experiment with local vegetables. The vegetables are both musical and useful: at the end of the performance, they make vegetable soup and serve it to the audience.

Glenn Donnellan is a classical musician who plays violin in the National Symphony Orchestra in Washington DC. As part of his job, he works with children. Sometimes young people think classical music is neither cool nor interesting so he wanted to involve them more. His answer was a Batolin: a violin made from a baseball bat. He made it from a normal baseball bat using tools that he found in the theatre where he worked. He says kids can make their own instruments. It is not only educational but also fun.

Mr Donnellan put a film of himself playing the Batolin on a video sharing website. Then he got a message from the Washington Nationals baseball team inviting him to play the national anthem before a match. The reaction of the crowd was extraordinary: they loved both the idea and the sound.

An award-winning composer, Bill Milbrodt, started the Car Music Project when his old car died. Instead of scrapping the car, he recycled it into musical instruments. He employed mechanics to take the car apart and a metal sculptor to make the instruments. He wanted to have traditional orchestral groups: wind, strings, brass and percussion. He also wanted the instruments to look like car parts but be like real ones so professional musicians can play them easily. The instruments include drums made from the wheels and a bass made from the petrol tank. Sometimes the musicians play music by composers but often they create their own sound, so the music Car Music Project plays can be either traditional or modern.

**5** Read the text again and choose the correct answers.

1 All the instruments in the article
   a) can be eaten.   b) sound terrible.
   c) are recycled.

2 The musicians in the Vegetable Orchestra
   a) like playing new vegetables.
   b) always make the same instruments.
   c) play songs about food.

3 At the end of a Vegetable Orchestra concert, the instruments are
   a) thrown away.   b) eaten.   c) sold.

4 Glenn Donnellan made his Batolin because he
   a) doesn't like violins.   b) is a baseball fan.
   c) works with young people.

5 Mr Donnellan put a film on a website _____ he played at the baseball game.
   a) before   b) after   c) when

6 Bill Milbrodt made his car into _____ instruments.
   a) rock   b) orchestral   c) percussion

7 The Car Music Project musicians
   a) make their own instruments.
   b) play different styles of music.
   c) are interested in cars.

**6** Look at the Word Builder. Complete the table with the adjectives in red from the text.

### Word Builder
| | |
|---|---|
| music | 1 _____ |
| use | 2 _____ |
| classic | 3 _____ |
| interest | 4 _____ |
| normality | 5 _____ |
| education | 6 _____ |
| tradition | 7 _____ |

**7** **Adjective Quiz** Work in pairs. Form adjectives from the words in the box and make sentences.

A  *electricity*
B  *electric. I'd like to play the electric guitar.*

| | | | |
|---|---|---|---|
| electricity | excite | experiment | aggression |
| power | relax | monotone | attract | logic |
| energy | mood | thought | enjoy | nerve |
| wonder | adventure | talent | artist | skill |

▶ Word Bank, pages 110–111

## Skills

**8** Look at the Sentence Builder. Which pair of linking words has a negative meaning?

### Sentence Builder

They are musical. They are useful.
They are **both** musical **and** useful.

It isn't cool. It isn't interesting.
It is **neither** cool **nor** interesting.

It is educational. It is fun.
It is **not only** educational **but also** fun.

They can play traditional music. Or they can play modern music.
They can play **either** traditional **or** modern music.

**9** Use the linking words from the Sentence Builder to join the sentences. There is more than one correct answer.

1 That music is beautiful. It is very romantic, too.
*That music is both beautiful and romantic.*
2 The concert was not interesting. It was not successful.
3 I like classical music. I like jazz, too.
4 Tonight we could go to the concert by Flo Rida. We could also go to the one by Tinie Tempah.
5 He can't sing very well. He can't play the guitar very well.
6 Avril Lavigne is a good singer. She is an excellent songwriter, too.

## Speaking

**10** Work in pairs. Ask and answer the questions. Is your partner musical?

1 Do you have music classes at school? Do you like them?
2 Can you read music? How well?
3 Have you got a good singing voice? What sort of songs do you like singing?
4 Can you recognise music from any classical composers? Which ones?
5 How many different instruments from an orchestra can you recognise? Which ones?

### Fact or Fiction?
The world's largest instrument is an organ in a cave in the United States. The 'stalacpipe organ' uses stalactites of different sizes to make different sounds.
— Answer on page 92. —

**TIMEOUT!** ▶ Page 103, Exercise 20

# 21 The Song

## Warm-up

**1** 🎤 **Speak Out** What is your favourite song at the moment? Which song do you really hate? Tell the class.

**2** What do you know about punk music? Answer the questions.
1. When did punk music start?
   a) the 1960s  b) the 1970s
   c) the 1980s
2. Which of these is not a punk group?
   a) The Ramones  b) The Beatles
   c) The Sex Pistols
3. Which were the most important punk cities?
   a) Paris and London
   b) New York and London
   c) Paris and New York
4. What did 'classical' punk fashion not have?
   a) spiky hair  b) baggy trousers
   c) body piercing

## Reading and Listening

**3** Read and listen to the dialogue. Check your answers from Exercise 2.

*The group have to work in pairs to give a presentation about a style of music. Then they perform a punk song.*

**Matt** I'm a bit nervous.

**Sam** It'll be okay when we start. Try to relax.

**Doug** Morning, everyone. Right, before the first version of the song, let's hear your presentation.

**Matt** Okay, right, you start, Jas.

**Jasmin** Well, our presentation is about punk. We like punk rock because the music is very fast and energetic. First, we're going to say something about the history of punk.

**Matt** Well, punk really started in about 1976. The Ramones in New York and The Sex Pistols in London were the most famous groups. In the late seventies, punk was big everywhere. It was less popular in the eighties but became popular again in the late nineties. For example, there were groups like Green Day.

**Jasmin** Okay, now let's look at punk fashion. Punks wanted to shock people. Both boys and girls had dyed, spiky hair. And face and body piercing were popular. Punks today still have spiky hair and wear leather jackets and old jeans with chains and boots.

**Matt** To finish, our opinion is that punk music is great but a lot of the fashion is pretty horrible!

**Doug** Right, thanks a lot. Now let's hear the song!

## Speaking

**4** Look at the Key Expressions. Which expression(s):

a) gives a reason?
b) introduces the presentation?
c) gives examples?
d) ends the presentation?
e) introduce a topic?

**Key Expressions: A Short Presentation**

1 Well, our presentation is about …
2 We like … because …
3 First, we're going to say something about …
4 For example, there were … like …
5 Okay, now let's look at …
6 To finish, our opinion is that … but …

**5** Read the Speaking Help.

**Speaking Help: Short presentations**

- Choose a topic you both like and know something about.
- Write notes for:
  the introduction (general information).
  first topic (e.g. the history of a style of music).
  second topic (e.g. fashion related to the music).
  the end (personal opinion).
- Decide which part of the talk each of you is going to give.
- Practise giving the talk. Use the Key Expressions.

**6** Work in pairs. Use the Speaking Help to prepare a talk about your favourite style of music. You can play a song from a CD or MP3 player.

**7** Give your talk to the rest of the class. Use the adjectives below to evaluate the talks.

- interesting/boring
- clear/confusing
- easy/difficult to understand

## Everyday Listening

**1** Look at the poster. Guess what kind of information goes in the gaps.

### West Lane High School
### BATTLE OF THE BANDS

1 _____ , 8th March  2 _____ – 8.00 p.m.

All bands and styles of music welcome.
To enter:
① collect a form from the school  3 _____
or
② enter online at westlanehighschool/competition.

All bands must enter by 1st 4 _____ .

Tickets (students £5 _____ , parents £6 _____ ) go on sale on 4th March. Drinks and 7 _____ will be for sale on the night.

**All profits go to charity.**

**4.10** **2** Listen to the conversation and complete the gaps.

**4.11** **3** **Listen closely** Listen to the introduction to a presentation. Identify the separate words in each sentence.

1 todayidliketotalkaboutthekindofmusicireallylikeatthemoment
2 iloveallsortsofmusicbutithinkthebestishiphop
3 areallycoolgroupistheblackeyedpeasfromla
4 theirlyricsarefantasticandilovedancingtotheirsongs
5 ivegotalltheiralbumsandiwatchtheirvideosonmtvwhenivegottime

TIMEOUT! ▶ Page 104, Exercise 21

# Across Cultures 4

## Warm-up

**1** Listen to the music. Work in pairs. Ask and answer the questions.
1 Do you like it? Why/Why not?
2 Where is it from?

**2** Look at the photos and the list of ideas. What do you think the text is about?
1 Caribbean dancing
2 Caribbean instruments
3 Caribbean music

## Reading

**3** Read the text and check your answer from Exercise 2.

### Where do calypso, dancehall, dub, garage, gospel, Hip Hop, R&B, reggae and steel drum music all have their roots? The Caribbean islands.

The Caribbean islands include the Bahamas, Barbados, Cuba, Jamaica and Trinidad. Most of the people in the Caribbean are descendants of West African slaves and settlers from Europe, India and China. Each island has its own music and in it you can hear the history of the islands. The African influence is in the use of drums, percussion and the style of singing. The European influence is in the use of instruments like guitars and the structure of the songs.

**Calypso** music is lively and it is played at carnivals when people dance in the streets. Sometimes it is played on an instrument called a 'pan' which is a steel drum made from an empty oil drum.

**Ska** is a fast dance music that comes from the late 1950s. Ska mixes American Rhythm 'n' Blues (R&B) with local rhythms. Ska bands play electric guitars and jazz wind instruments like trumpets, saxophones and trombones.

**Soca** started in the 1960s when a musician called Lord Shorty combined traditional calypso with classical Indian music. The word *soca* comes from **so**ul of **ca**lypso.

**Reggae** is slower than ska and it developed in the 1960s and 1970s in Jamaica. Usually a reggae band has electric guitars and drums. The lyrics are about local and political events and they are sung in Jamaican English.

### The influence of Caribbean music

is heard all over the world in modern music. Ska became very popular in Jamaica and south London in the 1960s. The first international ska hit was *My Boy Lollipop* which was sung by Millie, a Jamaican singer, in 1964. Bob Marley, another Jamaican singer, made reggae world-famous in the 1970s. Bob Marley's musical style was copied by British bands like UB40.
In the 1980s, music stars like Paul Simon, Peter Gabriel and David Byrne used Afro-Caribbean sounds in their music. The latest Afro-Caribbean singer to be internationally successful is the Barbadian R&B star, Rihanna.

**6** Use the Word Builder to complete the words in the sentences.

1. Millie was a Jamaic_____ singer.
2. In the past in Afric_____ , people used drums to send messages.
3. Europ_____ folk music often uses violins.
4. The Buena Vista Social club is a band which comes from Cub_____ .
5. Ravi Shankar plays an Indi_____ instrument called a sitar.
6. Harry Belafonte was the Americ_____ singer who made calypso music internationally popular in the 1950s.

## Speaking

**7** Work in pairs. Ask and answer the questions.

1. Where does your favourite music come from?
2. What are the titles of two good examples of the music?
3. Which instruments are used in the music?

**4** Read the text again. Are the sentences true (T), false (F) or is there no information (NI)?

1. ☐ The people of the Caribbean come from different countries.
2. ☐ All Caribbean music comes from Africa.
3. ☐ Calypso music started in the 1920s.
4. ☐ In the beginning, Calypso music used recycled instruments.
5. ☐ Ska music mixes different styles of music.
6. ☐ Reggae bands only use electric instruments.
7. ☐ The first international ska hit record was in the 1970s.
8. ☐ In the 1980s, Paul Simon used steel drums in all his recordings.
9. ☐ Rihanna comes from Barbados.

**5** Look at the Word Builder. Complete it with words from the text.

### Word Builder

| people | place |
|---|---|
| 1 | Africa |
| 2 | United States |
| 3 Barbadian | |
| 4 Chinese | |
| 5 Cuban | |
| 6 | Europe |
| 7 Indian | |
| 8 Jamaican | |

## PROJECT

### A biography

**1** Write the biography of a famous musician (classical or modern).

Find out information from encyclopedias, reference books and the Internet.

**2** Use the information to write notes in English about these things:

- family and early life
- early career as a musician
- the later or more recent years
- why he/she was/is important

**3** Use your notes to write a biography in four short paragraphs. Remember to include linking words.

**4** Work in groups. Read each other's biographies. Which is the most interesting?

# Study Corner 7

## Language Check

**1** What are the musical instruments?

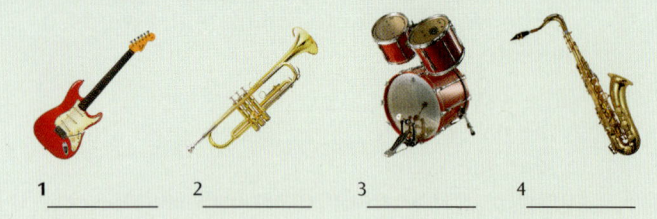

1 _____   2 _____   3 _____   4 _____

**2** Complete the sentences with the correct form of the words in brackets.

My sister is very ⁵_____ (music). She plays five different instruments.
My parents only listen to ⁶_____ (classic) music.
Most ⁷_____ (tradition) world music is very ⁸_____ (interest) because of the different instruments that are used.
Pop music is ⁹_____ (education), too! English songs are a ¹⁰_____ (use) way to learn new words.

Vocabulary ☐ / 10

**3** Choose the correct word.

11 Let's play *neither / either* dance music or R&B at the party.
12 *Neither / Both* Green Day and The Ramones are punk bands.
13 Classical music is not only interesting *but also / and* relaxing.
14 I was given neither a gift *nor / or* a card for my birthday!
15 Some people enjoy both traditional *or / and* modern music.

**4** Complete the sentences with *who, which, that, whose* or *where*.

16 What is the name of the city _____ The Ramones became famous?
17 Who is the composer _____ went deaf?
18 What is the wind instrument _____ is played by Native Australians?
19 Who is the singer _____ hit songs include *Material Girl* and *Like a Prayer*?
20 What is the city _____ The Beatles started?
21 Who was the man _____ invented the saxophone?
22 What is the style of music _____ is played by Green Day?
23 What was the name of the song _____ made the Arctic Monkeys famous?
24 What is the name of the singer _____ is called the 'Princess of Pop'?
25 What is the group _____ lead singer is called Bono?

Grammar ☐ / 15

**5** Complete the gaps with the words in the box.

| about   because   let's   like   something |

Our presentation is ²⁶_____ reggae. We like it ²⁷_____ it's great dance music. First, we're going to say ²⁸_____ about how it started. In the 1970s, it became popular around the world with singers ²⁹_____ Bob Marley. Okay, now ³⁰_____ look at some modern reggae singers.

Key Expressions ☐ / 5

## Feedback

- Listen and check your answers to the Language Check. Write down your scores.
- Look at the table. Check where you made mistakes.

| Wrong answers: | Look again at: |
| --- | --- |
| Numbers 1–4 | Unit 20 – Key Words |
| Numbers 5–10 | Unit 20 – Word Builder |
| Numbers 11–15 | Unit 20 – Sentence Builder |
| Numbers 16–25 | Unit 19 – Grammar |
| Numbers 26–30 | Unit 21 – Key Expressions |

- Now do the exercises in Language Check 7 of the Workbook.

## Study Help: English through songs

A good way of learning English is to listen to songs in English outside school.

You can find lyrics in pop magazines and on the Internet.

If you really like a song, read the lyrics and listen to the song several times. Work with a friend and translate any difficult words.

Remember, the grammar of songs is not always correct!

- Choose one of your favourite songs in English and follow the advice above.
1 Was the song easy or difficult to understand?
2 What new words or expressions did you learn?

# Module 8

- Talk about discoveries and inventions; make requests and offers.
- Read about giant prehistoric animals.
- Listen to a survey and a TV programme.
- Write invitation notes.
- Learn about unreal conditionals; *a few/few*, *a little/little* etc.

# Discoveries

## Get Ready

**1** Look at the Key Words. Which is the most interesting science? Which do you do at school?

**Key Words: Science**

archaeology  astronomy  biology  botany
chemistry  geology  medicine  physics
zoology

**2** Complete the sentences with the words in the box.

archaeologists  astronomers
biologists  zoologists

1 _____ discovered a new species of mammal in Borneo in 2005.
2 The discovery of the human genome by _____ has helped medical research.
3 In 1992, _____ used satellite technology to find the lost city of Ubar in Arabia.
4 In 2005, _____ discovered Xena, a new small planet in our solar system.

**3** Match the pictures (a–c) with the sentences (1–4) in Exercise 2. There is one extra sentence.

**4** Look at the list of important discoveries. Listen to three people talking about them. Which do they think were the most important? Why? Copy and complete the table.

- electricity • metals • new continents
- nuclear power • penicillin
- new planets and galaxies • radio waves
- vaccines • the human genome
- new species of plants and animals

| | Which discovery? | Why? |
|---|---|---|
| 1 | | |
| 2 | | |
| 3 | | |

**5** **Speak Out** Work in pairs. Decide what you think are the two most important discoveries in history and say why. Choose from the list or add your own ideas. Then tell the class.

*We think the discovery of the human genome was really important. It will change medicine in the future.*

## 22 Great Inventions

### Warm-up

**1** Look at the photos (a–d). When were these things first used? Check your answers on page 92. How did they change people's lives?

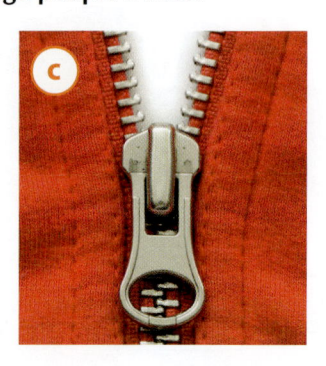

### Reading

**2** Read the text. Do you agree with the author's choice of inventions (1–3)? Which inventions (4–6) are most likely to happen?

**3** **Speak Out** What inventions would you like to see in the future? Why? Tell the class.

## What inventions have influenced our lives most? Here are my top three choices.

**1 Antibiotics**
Most of us would not be alive if doctors didn't use vaccines and antibiotics. Three centuries ago, people only lived until they were thirty-five years old and most of them died of infectious diseases.

**2 The Computer**
Frankly, my best friend – it plays games with me, plays music to me, helps me learn. I would lose contact with the world if my computer wasn't there on my desk.

**3 The Toilet**
Go ahead. Laugh. Then try to imagine New York City without toilets. If we didn't know how to remove sewage and bring clean water into buildings, modern cities wouldn't be possible. We would probably have cities but they would look and smell completely different.

And what about the future? When Leonardo da Vinci did a drawing of a plane, fifteenth-century scholars probably said: 'Forget it, Leon. If machines could fly, we'd know about it.' Perhaps some inventions that look impossible today will become reality one day.

**4 Teleportation**
Life would be much easier if we could just disappear in one place and reappear in another. Imagine how much time, money and energy we would save if we discovered how to get to foreign lands in a split second.

**5 A Universal Cure**
We can already cure most diseases but new ones are still appearing. If we found a universal cure, we could get rid of cancer and AIDS and face any future flu epidemic. Perhaps DNA research can help?

**6 Time Machine**
If we could travel in time, I'd definitely go and meet a few people from the past. Maybe it will be possible one day.

## Grammar: Unreal conditionals

**4** Match the sentences (1–2) with their meanings (a–b).

1) Most of us would not be alive if doctors didn't use vaccines and antibiotics.
2) If we found a universal cure, we could get rid of cancer and AIDS.

a) unreal, imagined present situation _____
b) unlikely future situation _____

**5** Complete the pattern with the correct tense and verb forms.

| Condition | Result |
|---|---|
| if + _____ | _____ /could (not) |

## Practice

**6** Complete the sentences with the correct verb forms.

1 If scientists _had_ (have) more money, they _could find_ (find) a cure for AIDS.
2 Water and air _____ (not be) so dirty if factories _____ (not produce) so much pollution.
3 If mobile phones _____ (not exist), we _____ (not be able) to talk to friends so easily.
4 We _____ (go) to the Moon if space travel _____ (be) cheaper.
5 If we _____ (can) write without pens or computers, we _____ (work) faster.
6 We _____ (have) more free time if robots _____ (do) our work.

**7** Match the conditions with the results. Write conditional sentences.

*1–e If we didn't have email, we would write letters.*

| Condition | Result |
|---|---|
| 1 we have email | a) it is difficult to communicate |
| 2 we use the Internet to find information | b) cloning is possible |
| 3 we can't prevent natural disasters | c) we don't go to libraries very often |
| 4 we have electricity | d) we use vacuum cleaners and dishwashers |
| 5 scientists know the genetic code | e) we don't write letters |
| 6 people don't speak one language | f) many people die |

## Your Turn

**8** Write sentences about what our life would be like without the things in the box.

*If I didn't have the telephone, I couldn't talk to my friends so often.*

bottles  CDs  planes  television
running water  cameras  remote control
guns  plastic bags  lifts  telephone

**9** Work in groups. Imagine how our lives would change if these things became true in the future. Make sentences about the consequences of each situation.

*If someone discovered a fountain of youth,*
*… they wouldn't tell anyone about it.*
*… they would sell it for a fortune.*
*… everybody would like to drink from it.*

1 Someone discovers a fountain of youth.
2 People invent a time machine.
3 People construct a spaceship that can travel as fast as light.
4 Aliens land on Earth.
5 The Sun is used as the only source of power.

**TIMEOUT!** ▶ Page 105, Exercise 22

# 23 Land of Giants

## Warm-up

**1** Look at the Key Words and answer the questions (1–5). Check your answers on page 92.

**Key Words: Animals**

crocodile   dinosaur   elephant   giant sloth
hamster   horse   lizard   mammoth
rhinoceros   sabre-toothed tiger   whale   wolf

1 Which animals don't exist now?
2 Which is the biggest?
3 Which is the smallest?
4 Which animals eat or ate meat?
5 Which can you keep as pets?

## Reading

**2** Read the text and identify the animals in the pictures (a–d).

**3** Look at the Reading Help.

**Reading Help: Identifying the main point**

- Look for one or two sentences in each paragraph with the main meaning. They are often (but not always) at the beginning of the paragraph.
- The main point is usually general and is supported with specific information and examples.

When dinosaurs dominated the Earth, mammals were small, furry animals, hiding in the forests. After the disappearance of the dinosaurs, these creatures evolved into modern mammals. But that isn't the whole story. Between the time of the dinosaurs and our own history, there was another time …

# A TIME THE WORLD FORGOT

**1** Fossils found in Germany show the existence of mammals about forty-five million years ago. One animal was an early relation of the horse but only fifty centimetres tall. **Ambulocetus** was even more amazing; it was a kind of small whale with legs, which probably walked and swam like a crocodile.

**2** In this period, birds were much bigger and more dominant than mammals. They probably developed from dinosaurs. Archaeologists have found evidence of huge birds like the **gastornis**. They were up to three metres tall and couldn't fly. They were meat-eaters – and there were lots of small mammals on the menu!

**3** When the Earth's climate got a lot colder, these giant birds died out and mammals took control but there's a big difference between these mammals and the ones we know today. The Earth thirty million years ago was a land of giant mammals such as a nine-metre-long rhinoceros and a five-metre-long wolf!

**4** The reason for the extinction of these giant mammals is a mystery but some were alive until quite recently. For example, we know early humans hunted mammoths and **sabre-toothed tigers**. And in the 1830s, Charles Darwin found the bones of a **giant sloth** in Chile which lived 10,000 years ago. It was the size of an elephant and looked like a huge hamster!

**5** Is this the complete story of the evolution of life on Earth? Probably not. We are discovering new information all the time. In 2005, Chinese scientists reported the discovery of a fossil of great importance. This unknown mammal lived about 130 million years ago and was a bit bigger than a cat. Interestingly, it had the bones of a small dinosaur in its stomach. A dinosaur-eating mammal? What will we discover next?!

# Skills

**4** Use the advice in the Reading Help to identify the main point in paragraphs 1–5.

1. a) Some fossils were found in Germany.
   b) Small mammals lived forty-five million years ago.
   c) Some mammals could swim.
2. a) Huge meat-eating birds dominated at this time.
   b) Birds evolved from dinosaurs.
   c) There were a lot of birds that couldn't fly.
3. a) The world got colder.
   b) Giant birds died out.
   c) Giant mammals became dominant.
4. a) Some giant mammals lived recently.
   b) Darwin made important discoveries.
   c) A giant sloth was the size of an elephant.
5. a) One mammal ate dinosaurs.
   b) Chinese scientists found a fossil.
   c) Scientists are discovering new species all the time.

**5** Are the statements true (T), false (F) or is there no information (NI)?

1. ☐ Archaeologists found fossils near Frankfurt in the 1990s.
2. ☐ Early horses were smaller than modern horses.
3. ☐ The ambulocetus was a type of crocodile.
4. ☐ Mammals dominated the animal kingdom forty-five million years ago.
5. ☐ Archaeologists have found the teeth of the giant wolf.
6. ☐ Humans lived at the same time as mammoths.

**6** Look at the Word Builder. Complete it with more examples of nouns in **blue** from the text.

### Word Builder

| -ry   | discove**ry**<br>1 _____ |
|-------|-------------------------------|
| -tion | rela**tion**<br>2 _____<br>3 _____<br>4 _____ |
| -ance | disappear**ance**<br>5 _____ |
| -ence | exist**ence**<br>6 _____<br>7 _____ |
| -ist  | archaeolog**ist**<br>8 _____ |

**7** Complete the sentences with words from Exercise 6.

1. The origins of life on Earth are still a _____.
2. Charles Darwin published his theory of _____ in 1859.
3. We think a change in climate caused the _____ of the giant birds.
4. _____ and _____ are finding new _____ all the time.
5. The recent _____ in China surprised scientists.
6. The dog is a _____ of the wolf.

**8 Game** Make nouns from the words in the box. Which is the odd-one-out?

| celebrate   explore   inform   prepare present   recover |
|---|

▶ Word Bank, page 110

**9** Look at the Sentence Builder.

### Sentence Builder

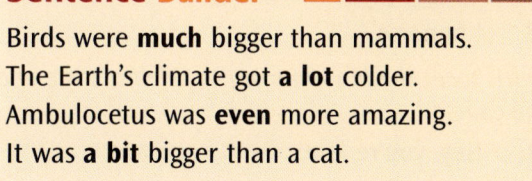

Birds were **much** bigger than mammals.
The Earth's climate got **a lot** colder.
Ambulocetus was **even** more amazing.
It was **a bit** bigger than a cat.

**10** Compare the animals in pictures (a–d). Use these adjectives.

- strange • colourful • dangerous • big
- small • interesting

*The ambulocetus is even stranger than the giant sloth!*

## Speaking

**11** Work in pairs. Find out about two more giant mammals.

▶ Student A, page 89
▶ Student B, page 90

### Fact or Fiction?

Archaeologists have found fossils of a giant pig. It was two metres tall and weighed 350 kilogrammes.
— Answer on page 92. —

**TIMEOUT!** ▶ Page 105, Exercise 23

83

# 24 A Surprise

## Warm-up

**1** Look at the photo. What do you think they are happy about?

- finishing the course • Jasmin's birthday
- passing an exam • Matt getting an audition

## Reading and Listening

**2** Read and listen to the dialogue. Check your guesses from Exercise 1.

*The course has finished. Gwen and Jasmin are going out when they meet Mr Bywater.*

**Gwen** Oh, here's Mr Bywater.
**Mr B** It's lucky I saw you. Are you seeing Matt tonight?
**Jasmin** Yes.
**Mr B** Can you do me a favour?
**Jasmin** Sure.
**Mr B** I'd like you to give him this letter.
**Jasmin** Okay, I'll do that.
**Gwen** Mm, sounds interesting.
**Mr B** I hope so.

*The girls meet the boys in town to celebrate the end of the course.*

**Matt** Hey, you're late!
**Gwen** Jasmin's got something for you.
**Jasmin** Yeah, Bywater gave me this letter.
**Matt** Bywater? What does he want?
**Jasmin** I don't know. Shall I open it for you?
**Matt** No, I'll do it.
**Sam** Come on, don't keep us in suspense.
**Matt** I don't believe it! Bywater recommended me to his friend. He's a film director in the States. I've got an audition next month for a small part in a film!
**Jasmin** That's brilliant!
**Gwen** Wow!
**Sam** And you never liked him!
**Matt** Well, I was wrong about him.
**Gwen** Okay. Come on everybody, let's celebrate!

**3** Answer the questions.

1 Why does Mr Bywater say 'It's lucky I saw you'?
2 What does Mr Bywater ask the girls to do?
3 How did Mr Bywater help Matt?
4 Why does Matt say 'Well, I was wrong about him'?

## Speaking

**4** Look at the Key Expressions. Which are requests (R) and which are offers (O)?

> **Key Expressions:** Offers and Requests
>
> 1 Can you do me a favour? *R*
> 2 I'd like you to give this letter to him.
> 3 Okay, I'll do that.
> 4 Shall I open it for you?

**5** Work in pairs. Take turns to ask favours. Use the ideas below.

- record the match tonight • help organise my party • lend me a couple of CDs • give my homework to our teacher • post this letter
- look after my hamster while I'm on holiday

**A** *Can you do me a favour?*
**B** *Sure.*
**A** *I'd like you to record the match tonight.*
**B** *Okay, I'll do that.*

**6** Work in pairs. Take turns to make offers. Use the ideas below.

- your friend has got two heavy bags
- it's warm in the room • your friend is hungry • the TV is very loud • your friend can't do his/her homework

*Would you like me to help you?*
*Shall I help you with your bags?*

84

# Skills

## Everyday Listening 🔊

**1** Listen to the TV programme. Choose the correct answers, a), b) or c).

1 Colin is …
   a) sixteen.   b) seventeen.   c) eighteen.
2 Colin is from …
   a) England.   b) Ireland.   c) Scotland.
3 Colin's invention is for children with …
   a) breathing problems.   c) learning problems.
   b) hearing problems.
4 The child breathes the spray through the elephant's …
   a) mouth.   b) tail.   c) trunk.
5 Who suffers from asthma?
   a) Colin's mother.   c) Colin's brother.
   b) Colin's cousin.

**2 Listen closely** Listen and complete the gaps with contractions.

1 And now _____ time for *Invention of the Week*.
2 Let us know and _____ try to help you.
3 Now, _____ Colin's invention.
4 _____ made a bag.
5 _____ connected to the elephant's trunk.
6 _____ got a little cousin.
7 And _____ been really successful.
8 _____ buy one if my son had asthma.

**3** Listen again and repeat the sentences.

TIMEOUT! ▶ Page 105, Exercise 24

# Your Challenge

## Writing: Emails

**1** Read the emails (a–c) and match them with the replies (1–4). There is one extra reply.

**a**
date Wed, 7th March 2012
to Sam
subject Galactic Wars

Hi Sam,
Can I borrow your copy of *Galactic Wars*? I've heard it's a really good game and I'm bored with all of mine. Could you bring it tomorrow ¹_____ I can play it at the weekend?
Thanks, Damian

**b**
date Wed, 7th March 2012
to Liz
subject Electricity equations

Hi Liz,
Can you do me a favour? I don't understand those equations on electricity ²_____ I can't do my physics homework. Can I come round to your house later this evening ³_____ you can explain them?
Tim

**c**
date Wed, 7th March 2012
to Sue
subject Jacket shopping

Hi Sue,
I've got to go shopping this weekend ⁴_____ get a new jacket. I need it ⁵_____ there's a family wedding next month and my mum has let me choose one myself. Can you come with me ⁶_____ help? We could go to that shopping centre. My mum can take us – she could pick us up outside your house at ten.
Emma

**1**
Okay, I'll come with you. I'd like to go there as well ⁷_____ get a new mobile phone. I'll see you then.

**2**
Sorry, I can't bring it in tomorrow ⁸_____ I lent it to my cousin. Would you like me to bring in some others? I've got a really cool one about aliens.

**3**
I'm really sorry but I can't come. I have to help my mum with the shopping on Thursday.

**4**
Sure, no problem. Come round at nine and we'll look at them together.

## Text Builder

**2** Complete the gaps in Exercise 1 with these linking words: *so, so that, to, because.*

1  so or so that

**3** Find the words in blue in the emails. What do they refer to?

'it' (a) – the computer game (Galactic Wars)

**4** Write an email to a friend.

**STEP 1** Write an email to a friend, asking for something.
• ask him/her a favour (e.g. to help you/to lend you something)
• give reasons

**STEP 2** Work in pairs. Read your partner's email and write a reply.
• say you can/can't do the favour
• if you can't, give reasons
• if you can, arrange when/how to do it

# Understanding Grammar: *a lot of/lots of, much/many, a little/little, a few/few*

**1** Read the text about Pompeii. Why do you think the volcano killed so many people?

> The Roman city of Pompeii was buried under volcanic ash when Vesuvius erupted in 79 AD.
>
> Before the explosion, Pompeii was a rich town, with 20,000 residents. The houses had running water and central heating. People who had **a lot of** money collected works of art. Pompeii had pavements, **a few** public baths and **lots of** shops. People lived happily, with **few** worries and **a lot of** hopes for the future.
>
> There were **a lot of** signs of volcanic activity but because they caused **little** damage, people didn't pay **much** attention to them. They felt safe and didn't expect any danger. On 24th August, they saw lots of smoke coming from Vesuvius but **very few** people understood what was happening. In fact, they had **very little** time to escape.
>
> A cloud of gas and ash fell down on the town and killed many people in **a few** seconds (the temperature of the cloud was almost 500°C). **A lot of** people suffocated – even **a little** volcanic ash and gas can kill immediately. Pompeii was buried under the ash for centuries until it was accidentally rediscovered in the eighteenth century.

**2** Compare the two columns below. Which of the words in **bold** are used:

a) only with plural countable nouns?
b) only with uncountable nouns?
c) with both uncountable and plural countable nouns?

| Countable nouns | Uncountable nouns |
| --- | --- |
| many people | much attention |
| a few seconds | a little volcanic ash |
| very few people | very little time |
| few worries | little damage |
| a lot of signs | a lot of money |
| lots of shops | lots of smoke |

**3** Translate the pairs of sentences into your language. Do the expressions in **bold** mean the same?

a) The earthquake caused **little** damage.
b) The earthquake caused **a little** damage.
c) The people had **few** worries.
d) The people had **a few** worries.

**4** Read the sentences and complete the rule with *many/much* or *a lot of*.

1 There were **a lot of** signs of volcanic activity.
2 People who had **a lot of** money collected art.
3 Were there **many** people who escaped?
4 Did the volcano produce **much** lava?
5 People didn't pay **much** attention to the signs.
6 Vesuvius didn't erupt **many** times.

> We usually use _____ in statements and use _____ and _____ in questions and negative sentences.

**5** Which response is more appropriate?

1 'There are thirty seconds left to the end of the match.'
 a) There's little time to score another goal.
 b) There's a little time to score another goal.
2 'I feel depressed and lonely.'
 a) It's because you have few friends.
 b) It's because you have a few friends.

**6** Choose the correct words. In one sentence, both options are correct.

1 There are *a few / a little* active volcanoes in the world.
2 We have *little / few* knowledge about other galaxies.
3 There are *a lot of / much* old Indian ruins in Latin America.
4 We don't like watching TV. We watch very *little / few* programmes.
5 Archaeologists don't find *a lot of / many* new historic places nowadays.
6 Europeans had *a little / little* gold in the sixteenth century so it was very expensive.
7 There are *very few / a few* archaeological sites in Antarctica.

**7** Look at your classroom and use these phrases to describe it.

There are a lot of …
There aren't many …
There isn't much …
There are very few …
There is very little …
There are a few …
There is a little …

87

# Study Corner 8

## Language Check

**1** Match the sciences (a–e) with the discoveries (1–5).

a) archaeology   c) botany   e) zoology
b) astronomy   d) medicine

1  A vaccine for polio – 1952.
2  New type of kangaroo in Australia – 1967.
3  Evidence of water on the planet Mars – 2000.
4  An ancient 'city of the dead' in Egypt – 2005.
5  Unknown plants in New Guinea – 2006.

**2** What are the animals?

6 _____   7 _____   8 _____
9 _____   10 _____

**3** Make nouns from the words in brackets.

Mars has always been a [11]_____ (mysterious) to scientists. In 2000, a *Mars Surveyor* spacecraft found possible [12]_____ (evident) of water on the planet. In 2004, after the [13]_____ (disappear) of *Beagle 2*, NASA sent two robots called *Spirit* and *Opportunity* to the planet. They sent a lot of important [14]_____ (inform) about the 'red planet' back to Earth, including an amazing [15]_____ (discover) – rocks from an ancient sea!

Vocabulary ☐ / 15

**4** Put the verbs in brackets in the correct tense.

If spaceships [16]_____ (go) faster, we [17]_____ (can) travel to other planets easily.

What period of history [18]_____ you (choose) if time travel [19]_____ (be) possible?

If we [20]_____ (not use) so much energy we [21]_____ (stop) climate change.

**5** Complete the gaps with the words in the box.

| few   little   many   much |

22 There are only a _____ mountain gorillas left in the wild.
23 Because of climate change, some areas of the world haven't got _____ water.
24 Pluto and Xena only receive a _____ light from the Sun.
25 Once there were _____ dinosaurs on Earth.

Grammar ☐ / 10

**6** Complete the gaps with one word.

A  I can't do this.
B  [26]_____ you like me to show you?
C  Can you [27]_____ me a favour?
D  Maybe.
C  I'd [28]_____ you to give this to Gary.
D  Sure, [29]_____ do that.

E  I can't open this packet.
F  [30]_____ I open it for you?

Key Expressions ☐ / 5

## Feedback

🔊 4.24
- Listen and check your answers to the Language Check. Write down your scores.
- Look at the table below. Check where you made mistakes.

| Wrong answers: | Look again at: |
| --- | --- |
| Numbers 1–5 | Get Ready – Key Words |
| Numbers 6–10 | Unit 23 – Key Words |
| Numbers 11–15 | Unit 23 – Word Builder |
| Numbers 16–21 | Unit 22 – Grammar |
| Numbers 22–25 | Understanding Grammar |
| Numbers 26–30 | Unit 24 – Key Expressions |

- Now do the exercises in Language Check 8 of the Workbook.

## Study Help: Self-assessment

- Which were the easiest and most difficult reading and listening exercises in this module?
- Look at your scores in all the Language Checks. What do you need to revise?
- Look at your portfolio. What are your weak areas in writing – spelling, punctuation, linking words?
- Look at the objectives boxes in the Get Ready sections. How well can you do the activities now? List the activities and give yourself a score.

*make suggestions: 7/10; write an email: 6/10*

# Student A

## Understanding Grammar, Exercise 6, page 27

Change the statements into questions by adding question tags. Add three questions of your own.

1  Your friends aren't fit, _____ ?
2  You like jogging, _____ ?
3  You learnt to ski in primary school, _____ ?
4  You can't swim, _____ ?
5  You've watched some sports competitions lately, _____ ?
6  _____
7  _____
8  _____

## Unit 7, Exercise 10, page 31

Use the cues to make passive questions. Then test your partner (the answers are in brackets).

1  What animal / used / as a symbol of medicine? (a snake)
2  When / plasters / invented? (1921)
3  What food / our teeth / most damaged by? (sweets)
4  Where and when / first glasses / invented? (Italy, 1285)
5  How many people / killed / by Spanish flu in 1918? (20–40 million)

Now try to answer your partner's questions. Choose answers from the box.

| South Africa, 1967    coughing and sneezing |
| 1895    a virus    plants |

## Unit 11, Exercise 11, page 43

**Roleplay 1**
It is eleven o'clock on a Saturday night. You are a parent. Your fifteen-year-old son/daughter is out with friends. You think he/she went to a youth club but you are not sure. He/she has got a mobile phone. He/she usually comes home about ten o'clock. You are worried. Then he/she comes through the door.

You start, e.g. *Where have you been*?

**Roleplay 2**
You are fifteen years old. You want to get a tattoo. (what part of your body?) Your parents won't let you. It is breakfast time and you are at the table with your mother or father. You raise the subject again.

You start, e.g. *Er, can I ask you something*?

## Unit 12, Exercise 7, page 45

You want to do these things at the weekend. Ask Student B to join you.

- go to the cinema   • play basketball
- go to an amusement park   • go for a walk
- cycle in the park

## Unit 13, Exercise 13, page 51

Use the ideas in the box to make questions. Add two questions of your own. Ask and answer the questions.

A  *Have you ever been abroad?*
B  *Yes, I have.*

- be abroad
- travel by ship
- meet a dangerous animal in the wild
- spend holidays on an island
- touch a snake

## Unit 23, Exercise 11, page 83

Read about these giant mammals. Ask and answer questions to complete the information.

Basilosaurus means 'King Lizard'. It lived _____ (*when*?) and looked like a whale. It was _____ long (*how long*?) and weighed sixty tons. They have found fossils in _____ (*where*?). Its head was as big as a sofa and it could eat _____ (*what*?)!

Smilodon means _____ (*what*?). Scientists have found bones and fossils of it in Brazil, Argentina and Bolivia. It lived over 100,000 years ago and looked like _____ (*what*?). It was two and a half metres long and weighed _____ (*how much*?). It killed horses and bison and ate the same as 120 burgers every day!

89

# Student B

## Understanding Grammar, Exercise 6, page 27

Change the statements into questions by adding question tags. Add three questions of your own.

1 You are quite fit, _____ ?
2 Your PE teacher doesn't play basketball, _____ ?
3 You can ski, _____ ?
4 Your parents taught you to swim, _____ ?
5 Our national football team hasn't won any matches lately, _____ ?
6 _____
7 _____
8 _____

## Unit 7, Exercise 10, page 31

Use the cues to make passive questions. Then test your partner (the answers are in brackets).

1 How / a cold / spread? (coughing and sneezing)
2 What medicines / used / in ancient times? (plants)
3 When / X-rays / discovered? (1895)
4 What / flu / caused by? (a virus)
5 Where and when / first heart transplant / do? (South Africa, 1967)

Now try to answer your partner's questions. Choose answers from the box.

| a snake   Italy, 1285   1921   sweets 20–40 million |
| --- |

## Unit 11, Exercise 11, page 43

**Roleplay 1**
You are fifteen years old. It is eleven o'clock on a Saturday night and you are going into your house. You went out at seven o'clock with your friends to a youth club. You usually go home about ten o'clock but tonight you are late. Why? Why didn't you phone your parents on your mobile?

Your mother/father speaks as you go in the door.

**Roleplay 2**
You are a parent. Your son/daughter wants to get a tattoo. You and your husband/wife don't want him/her to get a tattoo. It is breakfast time.

Your son/daughter raises the subject again.

## Unit 12, Exercise 7, page 45

Student A wants to do something at the weekend but you don't want to. Use these ideas to give your reasons.

- you don't feel well
- you've got a lot of homework
- it's cold
- you haven't got any money
- you have to babysit

## Unit 13, Exercise 13, page 51

Use the ideas in the box to make questions. Add two questions of your own. Ask and answer the questions.

B  *Have you ever travelled on your own?*
A  *No, I haven't.*

| • travel on your own<br>• read a travel book<br>• take a photo of a wild animal<br>• see a polar bear<br>• be to Africa |
| --- |

## Unit 23, Exercise 11, page 83

Read about these giant mammals. Ask and answer questions to complete the information.

Basilosaurus means _____ (*what*?). It lived about thirty-eight million years ago and looked like _____ (*what*?). It was twenty metres long and weighed _____ (*how much*?). They have found fossils in Egypt and the United States. Its head was as big as a sofa and it could eat sharks!

Smilodon means 'Knife Tooth'. Scientists have found bones and fossils of it _____ (*where*?). It lived _____ (*when*?) and looked like a big cat. It was _____ long (*how long*?) and weighed over 200 kilogrammes. It killed _____ (*what*?) and ate the same as 120 burgers every day!

90

# Questionnaire scores and answers

## Your talents. Exercise 4. Page 19.

True answers:

| | |
|---|---|
| 1 and 7 | You are good at using words. |
| 2 and 9 | You are a 'visual' person. |
| 3 and 10 | You are very musical. |
| 4 and 6 | You are a sporty and practical person. |
| 5 and 8 | You are very logical and good at maths. |

## How healthy is your lifestyle? Exercise 3. Page 29.

1  a = 0 points   b = 0 points   c = 5 points
2  a = 1 point    b = 3 points   c = 5 points
3  a = −20 points b = −5 points  c = 5 points
4  a = −5 points  b = 2 points   c = 5 points
5  a = −5 points  b = 2 points   c = 5 points

**Under 0** You really need to think about your lifestyle!

**0–10** Not bad but you must change some things!

**11–20** Your lifestyle is healthy but think about how you can improve it!

**21–25** Well done! You're very healthy.

### Reasons

1 Soft drinks have a lot of sugar in them and tea and coffee have caffeine in them.
2 To get the vitamins you need, you must eat five portions of fruit and vegetables a day.
3 Smoking greatly increases the risk of cancer and heart disease.
4 Physical exercise is good for the heart, muscles and circulation.
5 Teenagers should sleep about eight hours a night. Adults need less sleep.

## True or false? Exercise 11. Page 33.

1 It's unhealthy to drink a lot of coffee. **True.** Caffeine is bad for you.
2 It's bad to read in a room without much light. **False.** It can't damage your eyes but it can give you a headache.
3 It's dangerous to cycle without a helmet. **True.** You can get hurt!
4 It's good to drink milk before you go to bed. **True.** Milk has a chemical, tryptophan. When you drink it, you feel sleepy.

## Health quiz. Exercise 10. Page 37.

**1** c)  **2** b)  **3** c)  **4** a)  **5** b)  **6** a)

## How extrovert are you? Exercise 4. Page 39.

Most answers are 1: You are a very open and outgoing person – a real extrovert! You love being with people and meeting new people. Sometimes you 'speak before you think'!

Most answers are 2: You are a very sociable and friendly person. You enjoy the company of friends.

Most answers are 3: You are a quiet person and possibly a bit shy. You enjoy being with your friends but don't consider yourself a 'leader'. You are hard-working.

Most answers are 4: You are a very quiet and thoughtful person and possibly shy but you are not afraid to say what you think! You are hard-working and independent.

## How adventurous are you? Exercise 10. Page 53.

Most answers are **a)**: You are quite a careful person.

Most answers are **b)**: You are reasonably adventurous.

Most answers are **c)**: You are a real adventurer!

## Film and book quiz. Exercise 9. Page 63.

**1** c)  **2** b) and c)  **3** b)  **4** b)  **5** a)  **6** c)  **7** c)  **8** b)

## Music quiz. Exercise 8. Page 71

1 *Joaquin Phoenix*
2 What is the name of the female singer who has sold more records than any other woman? *Madonna*
3 Which boy band recorded *Lines, Vines and Trying Times* in 2009? *Jonas Brothers*
4 What is the name of the islands that/where reggae, ska and calypso music come from? *Caribbean*
5 What is the title of the album which/that is the biggest seller of all time? **Thriller** *by Michael Jackson*
6 What is the name of the singer whose song *Poker Face* was a hit? *Lady Gaga*

**Great inventions. Exercise 1. Page 80.**

| | |
|---|---|
| **matches:** | 1830s |
| **light bulb:** | 1880s |
| **zip:** | 1920s and 1930s |
| **credit cards:** | 1920s (in America) |

**Animal quiz. Exercise 1. Page 82.**

1  dinosaur, giant sloth, mammoth, sabre-toothed tiger
2  the whale
3  the hamster
4  crocodile, dinosaur, lizard, sabre-toothed tiger, wolf. Some whales also eat meat.
5  hamster, horse, lizard

## Fact or Fiction?

Unit 2, page 13, **fact**

Unit 5, page 23, **fact** (She won the Nobel Prize for physics in 1903 and later the Nobel Prize for chemistry in 1911.)

Unit 8, page 33, **fiction** (It takes the same time as other food.)

Unit 11, page 43, **fact**

Unit 14, page 53, **fact** (There are still about 50,000 lowland gorillas in central and west Africa. However, mountain gorillas are very rare and the population is declining.)

Unit 17, page 63, **fiction** (Steven Spielberg has only appeared once: as a tourist in *The Lost World: Jurassic Park*. Other directors have appeared in their films. The most famous is Alfred Hitchcock; he appeared in thirty-seven of his films. Peter Jackson had very small parts in each of *The Lord of the Rings* trilogy. Martin Scorcese also appears in many of his films.)

Unit 20, page 73, **fact**

Unit 23, page 83, **fact** (The enterodont lived twenty-five to forty million years ago. It was omnivorous and looked like a pig. Fossils were found in Mongolia and North America.)

## Irregular verbs

| Present Simple | Past Simple | Past Participle |
|---|---|---|
| be | was/were | been |
| become | became | become |
| begin | began | begun |
| bite | bit | bitten |
| break | broke | broken |
| bring | brought | brought |
| build | built | built |
| burn | burnt, burned | burnt, burned |
| buy | bought | bought |
| can | could | could |
| catch | caught | caught |
| come | came | come |
| cut | cut | cut |
| do | did | done |
| draw | drew | drawn |
| dream | dreamt, dreamed | dreamt, dreamed |
| drink | drank | drunk |
| drive | drove | driven |
| eat | ate | eaten |
| fall | fell | fallen |
| feel | felt | felt |
| fight | fought | fought |
| find | found | found |
| forget | forgot | forgotten |
| get | got | got |
| give | gave | given |
| go | went | gone |
| grow | grew | grown |
| hang | hung | hung |
| have | had | had |
| hear | heard | heard |
| hide | hid | hidden |
| hold | held | held |
| keep | kept | kept |
| know | knew | known |
| learn | learnt, learned | learnt, learned |
| leave | left | left |
| lend | lent | lent |
| lose | lost | lost |
| make | made | made |
| meet | met | met |
| must | had to | had to |
| put | put | put |
| read (/riːd/) | read (/red/) | read (/red/) |
| ride | rode | ridden |
| run | ran | run |
| say | said | said |
| see | saw | seen |
| send | sent | sent |
| speak | spoke | spoken |
| stand | stood | stood |
| swim | swam | swum |
| take | took | taken |
| tell | told | told |
| think | thought | thought |
| understand | understood | understood |
| win | won | won |
| write | wrote | written |

# TIMEOUT!

## 1 SCHOOL

Where do you do these things at school? Write the rooms or places.

1. go on the Internet

   c _ _ _ _ _ _ _ _  r _ _ _

2. play hockey

   h _ _ _ _ _  p _ _ _ _

3. do gymnastics

   g _ _ _ _ _ _ _ _

4. find things in an encyclopaedia

   l _ _ _ _ _ _

5. do experiments

   s _ _ _ _ _ _  l _ _ _ _ _ _ _ _

6. act or play music

   s _ _ _ _

## 2 Test Your Memory

What can you remember about the British boarding schools below? Draw arrows from the schools to the information.

It's for girls.    Pupils share rooms.

**ETON**

It's near the sea.    It's for boys.

**Roedean**

Pupils have their own rooms.    It's near London.

It's over 500 years old.

## 3 REPORTS

Read about these girls and write their names on the reports.

**Louise:** I love reading, especially fantasy books. I don't like maths much but I get quite good marks in exams. I hate physics and get terrible marks!

**Nikki:** I don't like reading much. I quite like science. I'm not very good at physics. I prefer chemistry and biology. I love biology and I want to be a vet.

**Ellie:** I'm quite good at English and I enjoy reading. But maths is my best subject and I get good marks in all the sciences. I want to be an engineer.

### 1

NAME: .................

| SUBJECT | % | COMMENT |
|---|---|---|
| English | 62 | Quite good but should read more! |
| Mathematics | 65 | Always works hard. |
| Physics | 53 | She could do better. |
| Biology | 72 | Shows a great interest in the subject. Well done! |

### 2

NAME: .................

| SUBJECT | % | COMMENT |
|---|---|---|
| English | 79 | Her writing is always interesting with very good vocabulary. |
| Mathematics | 77 | A very good exam but could work harder in class. |
| Physics | 48 | She isn't very interested in the subject. |
| Biology | 60 | Good work this term. |

### 3

NAME: .................

| SUBJECT | % | COMMENT |
|---|---|---|
| English | 72 | She always works with interest. |
| Mathematics | 89 | A very good student! A very high standard of work. |
| Physics | 76 | She shows a good understanding of all the work. |
| Biology | 81 | An excellent exam result and a very good project! |

# 4 WORD SEARCH

Find these adjectives in the word square. Look ↑ ↓ → ←

- artistic
- athletic
- creative
- imaginative
- logical
- musical
- practical
- talented

| I | M | A | J | A | T | V | E | P | E | T |
|---|---|---|---|---|---|---|---|---|---|---|
| V | A | L | O | R | P | I | V | R | T | A |
| E | G | O | R | T | A | T | I | A | I | R |
| I | M | A | G | I | N | A | T | I | V | E |
| D | U | L | O | S | A | V | A | R | E | R |
| A | S | T | A | T | H | L | E | T | I | C |
| T | I | V | H | I | L | E | R | L | G | O |
| O | C | L | A | C | I | T | C | A | R | P |
| T | A | L | E | N | T | E | D | E | A | R |
| A | L | O | G | I | C | A | L | D | C | A |

## 5 Talented Women

Here are the life stories of two talented women. The parts of each life story are in the correct order – but the stories are mixed up! Can you separate them?

Clara Wieck — A ☐ ☐ ☐ ☐ ☐
Anna Pavlova — ☐ ☐ ☐ ☐ ☐ ☐

**A** She was born into a musical family in Germany in 1819.

**B** She gave piano concerts when she was nine.

**C** She was born in Russia in 1881.

**D** She married the composer Robert Schumann in 1840.

**E** She went to a top ballet school in St Petersburg when she was ten.

**F** After he died in 1856, she became a music teacher.

Clara Schumann

**G** By the age of twenty-five, she had become the best ballerina in Russia.

**H** She danced all over the world and gave over 3000 performances.

**I** She gave lessons to many young musicians, including Johannes Brahms.

Anna Pavlova

**J** Her most famous dance was called The Dying Swan.

She died of pneumonia at the age of forty-nine.

**L**      She died while she was listening to one of
   **M** her husband's pieces of piano music.

## 6 Tenpin Bowling

Make words from the skittles and the balls.

Example logic + al = *logical*

How many words can you make? Write the words.

ic .................................................................

ive .................................................................

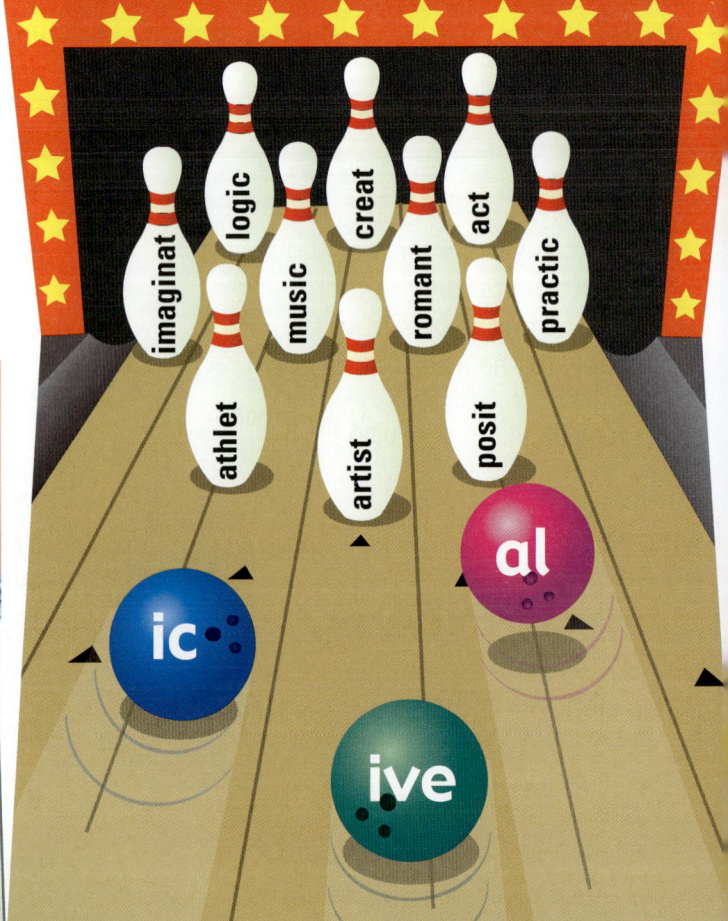

al .................................................................

Skittles: imaginat, logic, creat, act, athlet, music, romant, practic, artist, posit

Balls: ic, al, ive

94

# 7 MEDICAL QUIZ

**Choose the correct answers to the questions.**

1. Who is known as the 'father of medicine'?
   a) Hesyre of Egypt (2650 BC)
   b) Hippocrates of Cos (400 BC)
   c) Archimedes of Syracuse (287–212 BC)

2. When were false teeth first used?
   a) in Ancient Egypt in 2000 BC
   b) in Scotland in AD 1000
   c) in the USA in 1976

3. How were people infected with the bubonic plague (the Black Death)?
   a) by spiders
   b) by mosquitoes
   c) by fleas

4. When were bacteria first seen under a microscope?
   a) by Hippocrates in 402 BC
   b) by Anton van Leeunwenhoek in 1675
   c) by Einstein in 1928

5. Who discovered tuberculosis bacteria?
   a) the British scientist Charles Darwin in 1855
   b) the German scientist Robert Koch in 1882
   c) the Scottish scientist Fleming in 1929

6. When was an artificial heart first transplanted successfully?
   a) in 1982   b) in 2001   c) never

1b) 2a) 3c) 4b) 5b) 6c)

# 8 Odd one out

Find the odd one out.

**1**
a) bacteria
b) a virus
c) painkillers
d) an infection

**2**
a) an allergy
b) a sports injury
c) a cold
d) flu

**3**
a) vitamins
b) antibiotics
c) protein
d) minerals

**4**
a) an injection
b) a vaccination
c) yoga
d) antibiotics

**5**
a) AIDS
b) tuberculosis
c) mumps
d) vaccine

**6**
a) an X-ray
b) acupuncture
c) a herbal remedy
d) yoga

# 9 You're the Doctor!

**Match the diagnosis and treatment with the symptoms.**

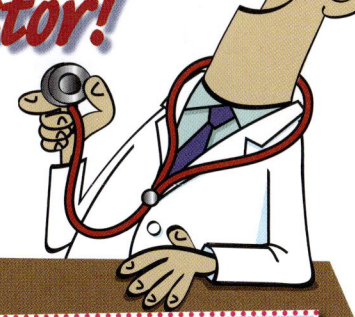

| SYMPTOMS | DIAGNOSIS | TREATMENT |
| --- | --- | --- |
| 1 'I've got red spots all over my body and a temperature. I don't feel hungry either.' | A 'You've got a cold.' | a) 'First, go and have an X-ray. Then come back and see me.' |
| 2 'I sneeze a lot when I'm near a cat. Sometimes it is difficult to breathe.' | B 'You've got flu.' | b) 'Take this cough mixture and three aspirins a day.' |
| 3 'I've got a really bad headache and a sore throat. I think I've got a temperature, too. I feel terrible!' | C 'I think you've got a broken toe.' | c) 'Don't go out because it's very infectious. Stay in a dark room and drink plenty of liquid.' |
| 4 'I fell over in the street and I've got a terrible pain just here.' | D 'I'm sorry but you've got measles.' | d) 'Don't go near cats and take some of these pills.' |
| 5 'I sneeze and cough a lot. I've got a bit of a headache, too.' | E 'You've got an allergy.' | e) 'Go to bed for a day or two. Take aspirins and drink a lot of liquid.' |

# 10 Who Are You?

How much do you have in common with your friends? Do this questionnaire. Then compare your answers with some friends' answers.

**1** The most important thing in a boyfriend or girlfriend is …
a) personality.
b) looks.
c) common interests.
d) intelligence.

**2** When I get home from school, the first thing I do is …
a) go on my computer.
b) do my homework.
c) open the fridge.
d) talk on the phone.

**3** I like listening to …
a) rock.
b) reggae.
c) rap.
d) anything.

**4** My ambition is to …
a) be rich.
b) find true love.
c) be famous.
d) get a good job.

**5** My bedroom is …
a) perfect.
b) quite tidy.
c) a bit untidy.
d) yuk!

**6** When I meet someone new, I first notice his/her …
a) eyes.
b) smile.
c) hair.
d) clothes.

**7** My favourite time of day is …
a) morning.
b) afternoon.
c) evening.
d) night.

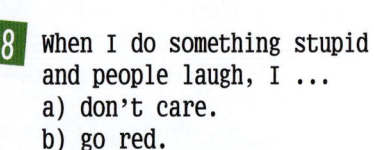

**8** When I do something stupid and people laugh, I …
a) don't care.
b) go red.
c) laugh with them.
d) get upset.

# 11 Diaries

Read the dialogues and diaries. Can you identify the boys? Write their names next to the pictures.

**1** How is your granddad?
Oh, he's okay. What's the new game like?
Brilliant.
**3**

**2** Did you go to the cinema?
Yeah, I went with Simon in the end. But it wasn't any good.
**4**

### 21 MARCH
I met Simon in town. He bought the new Narnia game. He invited me to his house but I had to go with my dad to visit granddad in hospital. Dad took me for a burger after the hospital.

### 21 MARCH
I went to the match with Sam. United were rubbish. We lost 2-0. Norton missed a penalty – again! Sam went home after the match. I went to the cinema with Simon. We saw the new Twilight film. Bit boring.

### 21 MARCH
I got the new Narnia game with my birthday money. I invited Paul round to have a game but he couldn't come because he had to visit his granddad. I played on my computer for an hour and then Peter phoned. We went to the cinema and saw the new Twilight film. It wasn't very good.

### 21 MARCH
United were playing Aston Villa. We lost. Really boring game. Peter wanted to go to the cinema but I didn't have any money. I stayed in and watched a film with my mum and dad.

# 12 Word wheels

How many personality adjectives can you make from the word wheels?

Examples
*friendly*
*unfriendly*

**PREFIXES**
out-
in-
un-
ex-
easy-

**BASE**
cheek
depend
friend
going
reli
thought
tid
trovert

**SUFFIXES**
-ent
-ly
-ful
-y
-able
-ed

Work in pairs. Compare your answers.

# Match-making

Match the people (1–4) with the best partner (a–d).
Who doesn't find a partner?

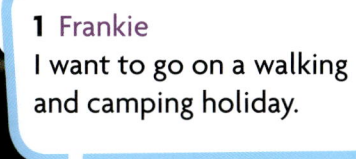

**1 Frankie**
I want to go on a walking and camping holiday.

**2 Nina**
I need to build a bookcase for my bedroom.

**3 Ali**
I need to revise with somebody.

**4 Alex**
I want to discuss my problems with a friend.

a Ana's hard-working, helpful and reliable.
b Danny's lazy, thoughtless and untidy.
c Jack's honest, kind and sensitive.
d Sophie's energetic, friendly and easy-going.

## 13 EXPLORER PUZZLE

Read the explorers' descriptions. Work out who they are. Write their names: Tim, Tom or Toby, under the drawings.

**A** Well, I've had a lot of adventures. I've seen lions in Africa, tigers in India and pumas in South America. I've crossed the Sahara desert on a camel and been on two expeditions in a sea kayak. I've done kayaking and whitewater rafting in Canada, too. That was great fun! I've already written three travel books and I'm writing another one now. I haven't been to Antarctica yet.

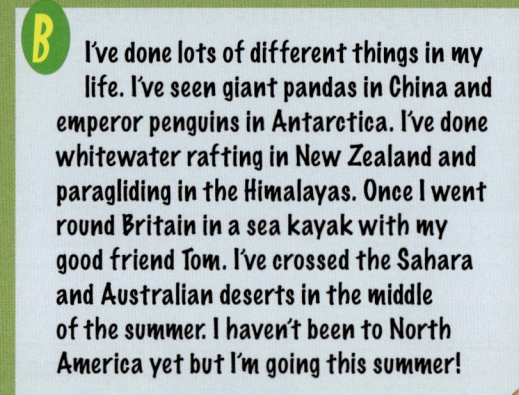

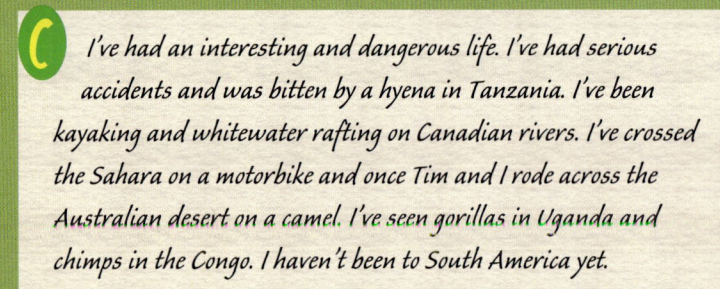

**B** I've done lots of different things in my life. I've seen giant pandas in China and emperor penguins in Antarctica. I've done whitewater rafting in New Zealand and paragliding in the Himalayas. Once I went round Britain in a sea kayak with my good friend Tom. I've crossed the Sahara and Australian deserts in the middle of the summer. I haven't been to North America yet but I'm going this summer!

**C** I've had an interesting and dangerous life. I've had serious accidents and was bitten by a hyena in Tanzania. I've been kayaking and whitewater rafting on Canadian rivers. I've crossed the Sahara on a motorbike and once Tim and I rode across the Australian desert on a camel. I've seen gorillas in Uganda and chimps in the Congo. I haven't been to South America yet.

## 14 Amazing but True

**Which one of these statements about animals is not true?**

1. A chimpanzee can recognise itself in a mirror but a monkey can't.
2. An iguana can spend twenty-eight minutes under water.
3. An albatross can sleep while it is flying.
4. Koalas are the noisiest animals in the world. You can hear them 3.5 kilometres away.
5. Mammals' blood is red, insects' blood is yellow and lobsters' blood is blue.

false = 4 The koala is not the loudest animal. The loudest animal is the howler monkey.

98

# 15 LET'S WRITE A POEM!

Read the poem. Which lines do you like best?

## TONIGHT AT NOON

Tonight at noon
Supermarkets will advertise
3p extra on everything

Tonight at noon
Pigeons will hunt cats
through city backyards
White Americans will demonstrate
for equal rights
In front of the Black House
And the monster has just created Dr Frankenstein.

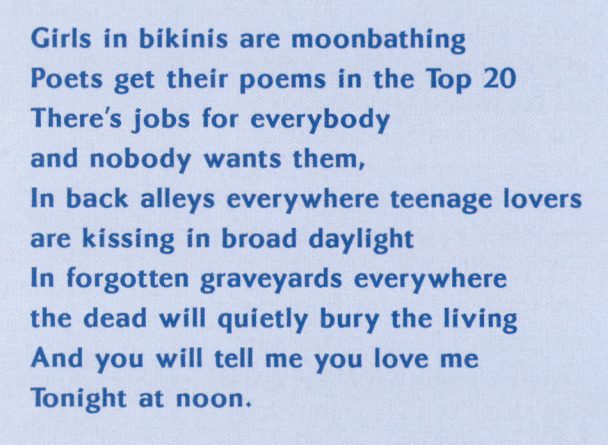

Girls in bikinis are moonbathing
Poets get their poems in the Top 20
There's jobs for everybody
and nobody wants them,
In back alleys everywhere teenage lovers
are kissing in broad daylight
In forgotten graveyards everywhere
the dead will quietly bury the living
And you will tell me you love me
Tonight at noon.

*Extracts from a poem by Adrian Henri*

Now try to write a short poem. Think of images, ideas and expressions which are the opposite of what you expect. This can shock, amuse or confuse the reader, like this:

I went into a slow-food bar and ordered a Small Mac with a hot cola.

I visited the zoo and saw thin hippos, a short giraffe, and a white widow spider.

Have you ever walked through hot, black snow on a dark summer's day?

Have you ever dived into an empty pool and splashed air onto everyone?

# ROMEO + JULIET

## 16 Capulets and Montagues

This story is based on Baz Luhrmann's modern film version of Shakespeare's play. Read the first part of the story and order the photos (a–c).

It is the end of the twentieth century in the American city of Verona Beach. The city is dominated by two rich families; the Montagues and the Capulets. They are terrible enemies. One day, three Montagues are at a petrol station when some Capulets arrive and there is a fight. Suddenly, a police helicopter appears and Captain Prince, chief of the city police, stops the fight. He takes the leaders, Mr Montague and Mr Capulet, to the police station and talks to them. If there is another fight, the people involved will get the death sentence!

Afterwards, the three Montagues go to the beach and meet Romeo, Mr Montague's son. He is sad because he is in love with a girl but she doesn't love him. The others laugh at Romeo. Later, Romeo and his friend Mercutio decide to go to a fancy dress party at the Capulet mansion. Romeo agrees to go, too because the girl might be there. At the Capulet house before the party, Mrs Capulet speaks to her daughter, Juliet. A friend of her father's, Dave Paris, wants to marry Juliet but she doesn't love him. The party is a success and after dinner the guests dance in the ballroom. When Romeo arrives he can't find his love but sees another beautiful girl dressed as an angel. They look at each other for a moment but her mother calls her. Later, they talk and kiss behind a curtain. The girl's old nanny finds them and the girl has to go upstairs – Romeo realises that the girl is Juliet Capulet! The nanny tells Juliet about him, too: 'His name is Romeo and a Montague – the only son of your great enemy!'

## 17 A Wedding and a Fight

Read the second part of the story. Find these things and places.

a) Romeo and Juliet get married here
b) they fall into it
c) the fight starts here
d) Romeo kills Tybalt here
e) the lovers hide here
f) Juliet arrives for the wedding in this
g) Juliet stands here after the party

After the party, Romeo goes into the garden and sees Juliet on her balcony. She can't see him and comes down to the swimming pool. There, she talks to herself about her love for him. Suddenly, Romeo jumps down from a wall, surprises her and they fall into the pool. At that moment, a security guard comes along and the two lovers hide underwater. After the guard leaves, they talk about their love. Romeo promises to organise a secret marriage.

The next morning, Romeo goes to see a priest, Father Laurence, and he agrees to marry the two young lovers that day. In the afternoon, Romeo is waiting in the church when Juliet arrives in a big, black limousine. Father Laurence marries them but they only have five minutes together before Juliet has to leave.

## 18 ETERNAL LOVE

**Read the last episode of *Romeo and Juliet*. Complete the review.**

| Review | |
|---|---|
| Favourite character | |
| Favourite part of the story | |
| Recommendation | *I recommend/do not recommend reading it.* |
| Why did you like/dislike it? | |

Later on, Romeo is on the beach with his friends when the Capulets arrive. Their leader is Tybalt, Juliet's cousin. Tybalt tries to start a fight with Romeo but Romeo doesn't want to fight his wife's cousin. Romeo's friends think he is afraid and one of them confronts the aggressive Tybalt. They fight and Tybalt kills Romeo's friend. When Romeo sees this, he gets angry and follows Tybalt in his car. There is a spectacular car chase through the city but Romeo finally catches Tybalt near an enormous statue. The police arrive but Romeo shoots and kills his enemy and then a friend helps him escape.

Finally, Captain Prince arrives at the scene and talks to everybody. Romeo must leave the city or face death!

After the fight, Romeo and Juliet meet and spend the night together. Romeo leaves early and goes to Mantua to escape from the police. Juliet's mother then tells her about the plans for her marriage with the horrible Dave Paris. The wedding is on Thursday!

Juliet goes to see Father Laurence. She wants to kill herself but Father Laurence has a plan. He is going to give her a drug. After Juliet takes it, people will think she is dead and will put her in the family mausoleum. Romeo will be there when she wakes up and they will go to live in Mantua. Father Laurence then sends a message to Romeo. Unfortunately, when the messenger goes to Romeo's flat, Romeo is listening to music and can't hear him. Back at the Capulet mansion, on the night before the wedding Juliet takes the drug. Everybody thinks she is dead and she is buried in the family mausoleum. One of Romeo's friends is there and he drives to Mantua to tell Romeo about Juliet's death.

When he hears the news, Romeo goes back to Verona Beach. He buys poison and then goes to the cemetery. He wants to die with Juliet. Father Laurence hasn't heard from Romeo and is worried. He drives to the cemetery, too. Two police officers see Romeo and his friend in their car and follow them. At the cemetery, there are police helicopters overhead but Romeo gets into the Capulet family mausoleum. He sees Juliet and thinks she is dead. He drinks the poison but then Juliet starts to wake up. They kiss and Romeo dies in her arms. Juliet then shoots herself. When the police arrive, they are lying in each other's arms, peacefully.

# 19 Did You Know?

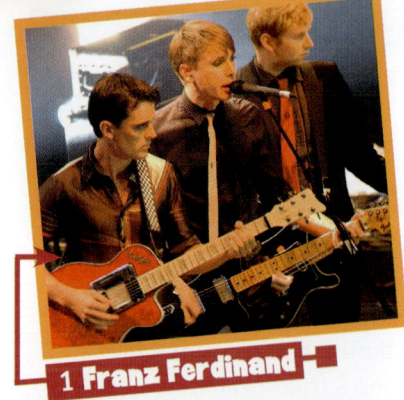

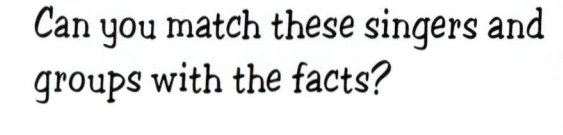

Can you match these singers and groups with the facts?

- [ ] a) He began his musical career in the group Take That.
- [ ] b) They were named after a racehorse.
- [ ] c) His real name is Marshall Mathers.
- [ ] d) She once starred in a hip hop version of the opera *Carmen*.
- [ ] e) They were named after a South African football club.
- [ ] f) His real name is Reginald Dwight.
- [ ] g) She wanted to be a ballet dancer.
- [ ] h) They changed their name from Starfish.

1 Franz Ferdinand
2 Kaiser Chiefs
3 Robbie Williams
4 Eminem
5 Madonna 
6 Coldplay
7 Beyoncé
8 Elton John

Answer Key: 1b) 2e) 3a) 4c) 5g) 6h) 7d) 8f)

# 20 Know Your Instruments!

Try this quiz.

**1** How many strings has a violin got?
a) three
b) four
c) five
d) six

**2** What is another name for the *mouth organ*?
a) harmonica
b) harmonium
c) harp
d) harpsichord

**3** Which of these is *not* a percussion instrument?
a) drum
b) oboe
c) tambourine
d) triangle

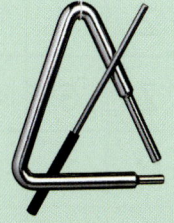

**4** What type of instrument is a Steinway?
a) guitar
b) piano
c) saxophone
d) violin

**5** What instrument are Eric Clapton, John McLaughlin and Paco de Lucia famous for playing?
a) drums
b) guitar
c) piano
d) violin

**6** Which is the largest string instrument?
a) cello
b) double bass
c) viola
d) violin

**7** What country does the balalaika come from?
a) Greece
b) Hungary
c) Ireland
d) Russia

1b) 2a) 3b) 4b) 5b) 6b) 7d)

# 21 jem

Read about Jem.
1. What was unusual about her singing career?
2. Why did she go to London?
3. Where did she have her first hit song?

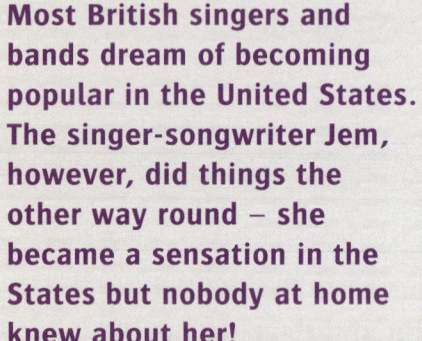

**Most British singers and bands dream of becoming popular in the United States. The singer-songwriter Jem, however, did things the other way round – she became a sensation in the States but nobody at home knew about her!**

Jemma Griffiths was born in Wales and started singing and writing songs when she was thirteen. She sang in small clubs while she was at university and then recorded her songs on a portable studio. She wanted to make an album, so the next step was London. She worked with a record producer but didn't make an album.

Jem decided to try the States. She recorded some songs in New York and sent 'demo' discs to radio stations. A DJ in Los Angeles started playing one of her songs, *Finally Woken* and it became a big hit. This led to a record deal and an album. In 2004, she appeared in teen American TV drama *The OC* and became famous internationally.

And what about her home country? In 2004, she returned to the UK and played her first show, a sell-out concert in London. Jem has never looked back.

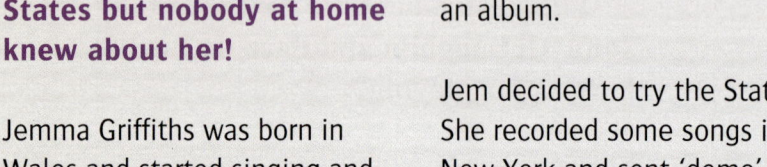

Find eleven styles of music in the wordsearch.

| H | E | A | V | Y | M | E | T | A | L | R |
|---|---|---|---|---|---|---|---|---|---|---|
| I | B | S | P | C | A | L | Y | P | S | O |
| P | U | I | S | L | E | V | A | X | P | C |
| H | H | R | J | A | M | T | P | U | N | K |
| O | N | E | S | S | Y | J | O | S | I | O |
| P | C | G | F | S | R | A | P | R | Q | P |
| V | W | G | E | I | S | Z | T | I | O | S |
| C | D | A | N | C | E | Z | S | X | B | M |
| N | T | E | S | A | L | M | T | K | Q | U |
| B | X | K | I | L | O | P | R | O | U | Y |

104

## 22 Amazing Inventions

Which one of these inventions (1–4) is scientifically impossible? Which one is a real product?

**1** *Clocky*

With 'Clocky', getting up in the morning is fun! When you press the 'off' button, Clocky moves off your bedside table onto the floor and hides somewhere in your bedroom. To stop the noise, you've got to find him!

**2** FIREPLACE WITH WATERFALL

This fantastic new fireplace doesn't only keep you warm. You can look at a beautiful waterfall in your living room and listen to the relaxing sound of water.

**3** Teleport

Do you hate the journey to school every morning? With 'Teleport' you can be there in a few seconds! Maximum range at the moment is five kilometres.

**4** Canine Diving Suit

Dogs love swimming but never get the chance to explore underwater. The next time you go scuba diving, take your dog with you in this fantastic new diving suit!

Real product: 1

## 23 INVENTED ANIMAL

Use the questions to invent your own creature. Compare it with your partner's.

**1** Where does the animal live?
 a) tropical rainforests
 b) polar regions
 c) the sea
 d) deserts
 e) big cities

**2** How much does it weigh?
 a) under 100 grams
 b) under 5 kilos
 c) under 50 kilos
 d) under 500 kilos
 e) over 500 kilos

**3** How does it move?
 a) it walks
 b) it flies
 c) it swims
 d) it jumps
 e) it doesn't move

**4** Which of these things has it got on or in its head?
 a) horns (like a reindeer)
 b) sharp teeth
 c) no teeth
 d) a beak (a bird's mouth)
 e) a long nose

**5** Which of these has it got?
 a) a long neck
 b) a tail
 c) long back legs
 d) claws (like a cat's fingers)
 e) toes or fingers

**6** What has it got on its body?
 a) fur (long or short?)
 b) skin
 c) scales (like a fish)
 d) feathers (like birds)
 e) shell or protective armour (like a turtle)

**7** What does it eat?
 a) bacteria
 b) plants and leaves
 c) insects and small animals
 d) big animals
 e) dead animals

**8** What sort of animal is it?
 a) a reptile
 b) a mammal
 c) an insect
 d) a bird
 e) a fish

## 24 Book Quiz

Which of the characters in the story . . .

1 ... lives in London? _____

2 ... wants to be a film director? _____

3 ... is allergic to cats? _____

4 ... are superstitious? _____ and _____

5 ... thought Mr Bywater was strange to start with? _____

6 ... is good at bowling? _____

7 ... was the cameraman in the film? _____

8 ... rescued Matt's wallet and passport? _____

9 ... like punk music? _____ and _____

105

# Word Bank

## Multi-part Verbs

**calm down** relax: *I was angry at first but I **calmed down** later.*

**come across someone/something** meet or find a person or thing by accident or by chance: *I **came across** my old passport in the drawer.*

**come in/into something** enter: *The students **came into** the classroom.*

**come round** visit: *My friends are **coming round** for dinner.*

**die out** disappear or become extinct: *Dinosaurs **died out** millions of years ago.*

**find out (something)** learn or discover a fact: *Did you **find out** the train times?*

**get away from** to leave or escape from a person or place: ***Get away from** that dog! He bites.*

**get into something** enter a vehicle or place: *They **got into** a taxi. They **got into** the building through the back door.*

**get in touch with someone** contact someone: *A friend of mine from primary school **got in touch** with me last week.*

**get off/on (something)** climb off/onto a form of transport: *I **got on** the train in London and **got off** in Birmingham.*

**get on with someone** be friendly with someone: *I **get on with** my cousin.*

**get (something) out (of something)** move a vehicle out of a place: *The car park was so full, it was difficult to **get** the car **out**.*

**get past (someone/something)** move past someone or something: *The lorry was wide and we couldn't **get past** it.*

**get together (with someone)** meet: *We often **get together (with friends)** for a chat.*

**get up** get out of bed: *I usually **get up** at 8.00.*

**go away** leave: *A lot of people **went away** from the match early.*

**go back** return: *I **went back** to my primary school last week.*

**go out (with someone)** spend time with someone in a romantic relationship: *Rob is **going out with** Sue.*

**look after someone** take care of: *Nurses **look after** patients.*

**put something on** put clothes on your body: *It was cold so I **put** my coat **on**.*

**put up something** build or assemble: *We **put up** our tent in the campsite.*

**take care of someone/something** look after: *My sister **took care of** my dog when I was away.*

**take part in something** do an activity with other people: *I **take part in** the school sports day every year.*

**take place** happen: *The party **took place** in a very big house.*

**take up something** begin a hobby or activity: *Rob and Jan **have taken up** golf.*

**turn somebody/something down** refuse an offer or invitation: *I asked her to go out with me but she **turned** me **down**. They **turned down** our offer.*

## Prepositions

### with adjectives

**allergic to** *I am **allergic to** seafood.*

**angry about** *My dad is **angry about** my results at school.*

**bad at** *My sister's very **bad at** singing.*

**bored of** *I'm **bored of** watching adverts on TV – they're really bad!*

**bored with** *I'm **bored with** this game. Let's play something else.*

**good at** *My mum is very **good at** painting.*

**pleased for** *I was so **pleased for** my sister when she passed her exams.*

**sick of** *I'm **sick of** being in traffic jams every day.*

**wrong about** *I was **wrong about** the time of the train.*

### with verbs

**argue about** *My sister and I **argue about** TV programmes.*

**charge for** *Most schools **charge for** trips and extra activities.*

**die of** *Rosalind Franklin **died of** cancer.*

**know about** *I **know** a lot **about** aeroplanes because my dad's a pilot.*

**learn about** *I'd like to **learn about** astronomy – I love the stars.*

**listen to** *I love **listening to** music.*

**live in** *The Brontë sisters **lived in** Yorkshire.*

**look after** *Will you **look after** my cat while I'm on holiday?*

**pay for** *She **paid for** her coffee and left the restaurant.*

**study for** *I'm **studying for** a maths exam.*

**think about** *I sometimes **think about** my grandmother's old house.*

**travel to** *Lady Mary Wortley Montagu **travelled to** Turkey.*

**wait for** *Sometimes, I have to **wait** twenty minutes **for** the school bus.*

**work on** *Crick and Watson **worked on** their DNA research for many years.*

**worry about** *I never **worry about** exams – I'm quite good at them.*

**write about** *Some authors **write about** their experiences.*

# Word Bank

## Word Families
### Cooking
**barbecue** cook outside on a charcoal or wood fire: *We **barbecued** kebabs at our garden party.*
**boil** cook food in boiling water: *Don't **boil** the vegetables for too long.*
**fry** cook food in a little fat or oil in a pan: *I love **fried** eggs and chips!*
**grill** cook under a grill without fat or oil: *Let's **grill** some fish for lunch.*
**roast** cook food in fat or oil in an oven: *Are you going to **roast** the chicken?*
**steam** cook with the steam from boiling water: *Vegetables are healthier when they are **steamed**.*
**stew** cook slowly for a long time in liquid: *We **stewed** pears for desert.*

## Confusing Words
**actually** in fact (<u>not</u> now/at the moment): *He is **actually** from Argentina, not Spain.*
**bring** carry or move something towards the person speaking: *Can you **bring** a newspaper from the shops?*
**carry** move something in your hands, arms or on your back: *I'll **carry** your bag for you.*
**earn** to get money by working: *Top footballers **earn** millions of euros.*
**journey** the movement to or from a place: *It's only a short train **journey** from London to France.*
**nowadays** at the moment: *More women go to work **nowadays** than in the past.*
**rob** take (steal) things from a person or place: *They **robbed** the old woman.*
**steal** to take an object that doesn't belong to you: *They **stole** the old woman's bag.*
**take** 1 carry or move something away from the person speaking: *Your dad forgot to **take** his bag to work* 2 help or move somebody/something from one place to another: *Can you **take** me to the station?*
**trip** a journey to a place and back: *We went on a two-week **trip** to the Lake District.*
**wear** have clothes on: *He's **wearing** a great jacket.*
**win** to be successful in a competition: *Do you think they'll **win** the match?*

## Compounds
### One-word nouns
**backpacker** a person (usually young) travelling with a backpack or rucksack
**birdwatching** watching and studying birds for a hobby
**bookshelf** a piece of furniture where you keep books
**campsite** a place where you can stay with a tent
**hardback (book)** a book with a hard cover
**laptop (computer)** a computer that you can carry around
**lifeboat** a boat that is sent out to help people in danger at sea
**lifestyle** the way people live
**lunchtime** the time in the middle of the day when people eat lunch
**nightlife** entertainment in a city at night
**paragliding** flying with a parachute
**phonebook** a book where you keep your phone numbers (also in mobile phones)
**rainforest** a tropical forest with tall trees
**seaside** an area or town by the sea
**sightseeing** visiting famous or interesting places
**skateboarding** riding on a small board with wheels
**snowmobile** a motor vehicle with tracks for travelling on snow
**timetable** list of times (e.g. for buses/classes)
**underground** railway that is underground (metro)
**weekday** Monday to Friday
**wildlife** animals and plants in natural conditions

### Two-word nouns
**4x4 vehicle** a car with four-wheel drive (rather than the more common two-wheel drive)
**boarding school** a school which the pupils sleep in
**bowling alley** a place you can go bowling (you have to knock down wooden pins with a heavy ball)
**box office** where you buy tickets for the cinema or theatre
**boy (girl) band** a pop music group with only boys (girls)
**camping equipment** things you need for camping
**chewing gum** a kind of sweet you can chew for a long time
**computer program** instructions to make a computer do something
**day school** a school where you go home after classes
**day trip** a trip somewhere and back in one day

# Word Bank

**e-book** a book in a digital format you can download and read on your computer

**film director** a person who directs a film (e.g. Hitchcock/Spielberg)

**fire engine** lorries that firefighters use to put out fires

**firefighter** a person who puts out fires

**forest fire** a fire that destroys trees

**generation gap** the difference in ideas and opinions between older and younger people

**high school** an American secondary school for 14–18-year-olds

**holiday resort** a town on the coast or mountains where people go on holiday

**luxury hotel** an expensive and comfortable hotel

**mobile phone** a telephone that you can carry around

**mountain gorilla** gorillas living in the mountains of Africa

**national park** a protected area of natural beauty

**nature lover** someone who is interested in nature and wildlife

**return flight** a flight to a place and back

**school holidays** time when schools are closed

**school lunch** lunch you have at school

**seafood** animals from the sea that you can eat – especially shellfish

**secret agent** a person who finds out secrets about other countries

**shopping centre** (US: shopping mall) a place with a lot of shops, cafés, cinemas

**special effects** unusual sound or image in a film that is made artificially

**table tennis** an indoor game played on a special table by two or four players who hit a plastic ball over a net

**tennis court** place where you play tennis

**tourist information office** a place to get information about what to visit and do in a city

**youth hostel** a place where young people can stay cheaply

## Two-word adjectives

**after-school** happening after the end of the school day (e.g. after-school club)

**air-conditioned** (room/house/car) kept cool by a machine

**centrally-heated** (house/office) kept warm by a machine

**computer-generated** made by a computer

**English-speaking** with the ability to speak English

**five-star** very good or luxury (hotel or restaurant)

**four-day** something lasting for four days (also three-day/two-day, etc.)

**good-looking** attractive (men and women)

**hard-working** a hard-working person works a lot

**long-haired** with long hair

**lovesick** spending all the time thinking about someone you love

**non-fiction (books)** books about facts or events

**open-air** not in a building (e.g. open-air concert)

**well-known** famous

**world-famous** famous all round the world

## Numbers

**twenty-one, forty-six, eighty-nine, etc.**
She's **twenty-two** years old.

## Verbs

**download** move things from the Net to your computer

**fast forward** to move a DVD, video or cassette forward

## Collocations

| Verb | Noun |
| --- | --- |
| cross | a bridge, a road |
| do | athletics, badly, calculations, somebody a favour, homework, household chores (e.g. washing-up), my best, a project, puzzles, the shopping, things together, tricks, the washing-up, well |
| earn | money |
| get | angry, a cold, fit, a message, a phone call, worried |
| get into | trouble |
| go | bowling, deaf, shopping |
| go by | canoe, helicopter, lorry, motorbike, mountain bike, paraglider, spaceship, tram, underground (metro), van, yacht |
| go on | foot, horseback |
| have | an accident, an argument, an illness, a meal |
| have (got) | an allergy, a cold, a cough, the flu, a headache, a pain in …, a sore throat, a temperature, a toothache |
| high/low in | calories, carbohydrates, cholesterol, fat, minerals, protein, sugar, vitamins |
| make | the bed, a cup of tea, a decision, an effort, a film, friends, a fuss, a mess, a mistake, money, a phone call, a suggestion, trouble |
| pay | attention (to something) |
| play | a musical instrument, a part in a play/film, a sport |
| put up | decorations, a tent |
| raise | money |
| save spend waste | money/time |
| see | the sights |
| share | a room |
| take | decisions, medicine, a message, somebody/something seriously |
| watch | a DVD, a film, TV |
| win | an award, the lottery, a medal, points |

| Adjectives | Noun |
| --- | --- |
| common | disease |
| dangerous | accident, snake |
| everyday | life |
| loud | noise |
| physical | exercise |
| popular | subject |
| private/extra | classes |
| rare | species |
| tasty | food, meal, snack |
| terrible | accident |
| traditional | activities, costume, dances, dress, lifestyle, songs, |
| wild | animal |

## Building

| Noun | Adjective | Verb |
|---|---|---|
| amazement | amazed/amazing | amaze |
| annoyance | annoyed/annoying | annoy |
| attraction | attractive | attract |
| care | careful | care |
| celebration | celebratory | celebrate |
| cheer | cheerful | cheer |
| creativity | creative | create |
| death | dead/deadly | die |
| depression | depressed/depressing | depress |
| difference | different | differ |
| disappearance | – | disappear |
| discovery | – | discover |
| enjoyment | enjoyable | enjoy |
| evolution | evolutionary | evolve |
| excitement | excited/exciting | excite |
| existence | – | exist |
| experiment | experimental | experiment |
| explanation | explanatory | explain |
| exploration | exploratory | explore |
| imagination | imaginative | imagine |
| information | informative | inform |
| interest | interested/interesting | interest |
| irritation | irritated/irritating | irritate |
| life | lively | live |
| poison | poisonous | poison |
| preparation | prepared | prepare |
| presentation | presentable | present |
| protection | protected/protective | protect |
| recovery | – | recover |
| relation | related | relate |
| relaxation | relaxed/relaxing | relax |
| reliability | reliable | rely |
| repetition | repetitive | repeat |
| scare | scared/scary | scare |
| success | successful | succeed |
| surprise | surprised/surprising | surprise |
| talk | talkative | talk |
| thought | thoughtful | think |
| use | useful | use |
| worry | worried/worrying | worry |

## Word Building Continued

| Noun | Adjective |
|---|---|
| adventure | adventurous |
| aggression | aggressive |
| archaeologist | archaeological |
| art/artist | artistic |
| athletics | athletic |
| beauty | beautiful |
| biology/biologist | biological |
| botany/botanist | botanical |
| classic | classical |
| danger | dangerous |
| domination | dominant |
| education | educational |
| electricity | electric |
| energy | energetic |
| evidence | evident |
| expense | expensive |
| extinction | extinct |
| fame | famous |
| fashion | fashionable |
| friend | friendly |
| fun | funny |
| geology/geologist | geological |
| height | high |
| history | historical |
| importance | important |
| logic | logical |
| medicine | medical |
| monotone | monotonous |
| mood | moody |
| music | musical |
| mystery | mysterious |
| nerve | nervous |
| normality | normal |
| physics/physicist | physical |
| power | powerful |
| romance | romantic |
| science/scientist | scientific |
| skill | skilful |
| strength | strong |
| talent | talented |
| tradition | traditional |
| wonder | wonderful |
| zoology/zoologist | zoological |

## Opposites

| | | |
|---|---|---|
| antibacterial | inconsiderate | uncomfortable |
| antiviral | incorrect | unfair |
| impatient | incredible | unfit |
| impolite | inexpensive | unhappy |
| impossible | inexperienced | unhealthy |
| | invisible | uninhabited |
| | | unkind |
| | | unknown |
| | | unlikely |
| | | unlucky |
| | | unnecessary |
| | | unpleasant |
| | | untidy |
| | | unusual |

111

...mited

...panies throughout the world.

...om

© Pearson Education Limited 2012

The right of Michael Harris, David Mower, Anna Sikonzyńska and Lindsay White to be identified as authors of this Work has been asserted by them in accordance with the Copyright, Designs and Patents Act 1988.

All rights reserved; no part of this publication may be reproduced, stored in a retrieval system, or transmitted in any form or by any means, electronic, mechanical, photocopying, recording, or otherwise, without the prior written permission of the Publishers.

First published 2012
Third impression 2013

ISBN: 978-1-4082-5838-5

Set in Ocean Sans
Printed in China
CTPSC/03

## Acknowledgements

*We are grateful to the following for permission to reproduce copyright material:*

### Text

Extract 1.1 adapted from UWC Atlantic College. Reproduced with kind permission of UWC Atlantic College, www.atlanticcollege.org; and Poetry 6.1 "Tonight at Noon" from The Mersey Sound, Penguin (Adrian Henri, 1967), copyright © 1967 Adrian Henri. Reproduced by permission of the Estate of Adrian Henri c/o Rogers, Coleridge & White Ltd., 20 Powis Mews, London W11 1JN.

In some instances we have been unable to trace the owners of copyright material, and we would appreciate any information that would enable us to do so.

### Illustration acknowledgements

Alan Rowe 6, 86, 94br, 95mr, 105;
David Semple 93, 95l, 98br, 99;
Debbie Ryder 76, 96l, 98t;
Oxford Designers and Illustrators 82;
Paul McCaffrey 61;
Roger Wade Walker 94l;
Tony Forbes 47

## Photo acknowledgements

The publisher would like to thank the following for their kind permission to reproduce their photographs:

(Key: b-bottom; c-centre; l-left; r-right; t-top)

**Alamy Images:** Catchlight Visual Services 42t, Tony Charnock 103c (Harmonica), Pavlos Christoforou 56b, Richard G. Bingham II 4r, i love images 40tl, Images-USA 11r, Janine Wiedel Photolibrary 16l, Jeff Morgan 07 12t, Peter Adams Photography Ltd 56t, Jeff Rotman 50b, David White 12b; **Aquarius Collection:** 20th Century Fox 100tl, 100tr, 100b, 101t, 101b; **Corbis:** 23, Amy C. Etra 20, Kai Chiang / Golden Pixels LLC 42b, Michael Kevin Daly 49tl, Reuters 62c, Nigel Roddis / Reuters 49c, Zero Creatives / cultura 10l; **DK Images:** 78cr, 78r, Garth Blore 78l, Demetrio Carrasco 103br (Balalaika); **Mary Evans Picture Library:** Henry Grant 22c, Interfoto 62r; **Fotolia.com:** felinda 80cr, Greenfire 32r, Ivanov 33r, JonRob 50t (Great Wall), khz 80r, Okea 36b, Alexander Raths 79r, runzelkorn 39br, Max Tactic 29bl; **Getty Images:** 22t, 69r, AFP 19cr, 76l, 79l, ATABOY 46, Jorn Georg Tomter 57t, Hayley Madden / Redferns 102tr, Clarissa Leahy 39c, Mick Hutson / Redferns 102bl, Neil Lupin / Redferns 102br, Phil Dent / Redferns 102bc (Madonna), Photodisc / Siede Preis 103t (Violin), Redferns 70tc, 70bc, 70br, Rob Verhorst / Redferns 102cl, Tabatha Fireman / Redferns 102tl, 104, Thinkstock 49bl, WireImage 19r; **iStockphoto:** AdamGregor 29br, Beboy_ltd 87, Nilgun Bostanci 36cr, Jani Bryson 4l, Steve Debenport 97tr, Lisa F. Young 76r, Ines Koleva 32c, Nicolas Loran 80l, NickyBlade 40tr, Franck Olivier Grondin 33l, Vicki Reid 41t, Stellajune3700 39tl, Evgeny Terentev 80cl, Joao Virissimo 36c, Paul Whitton 32l; **Kobal Collection Ltd:** Columbia 67t, Orion / Regan, Ken 67b; **Pearson Education Ltd:** Eyewire 103c (Tambourine), 103bl (Drum), 103bc (Triangle), Chris Parker 40b, Photodisc. Alan D. Carey 53, Photodisc. Buccina Studios 10r, Photodisc. C Squared Studios. Tony Gable 78cl, 103bc (Oboe), Photodisc. Malcolm Fife 57b, Photodisc. StockTrek 79c, Jules Selmes 39bl, 97br, Studio 8 5, 41b, 97tl, 97bl; **Pearson Education Ltd:** Gareth Boden 93tl, 93r, 93bl; **Photolibrary.com:** Jin Akaishi 50t (Reporter), Kevin G Smith 49br, Kablonk! Kablonk! 16r, Wolfgang Meier 52, Photodisc 11l; **Press Association Images:** Gail Burton / AP 72t, Julie Jacobson / AP 27r, Wei Zheng / ColorChinaPhoto / AP 27l; **Reuters:** David Bebber 72c, Jorge Silva 77; **Rex Features:** Andre Csillag 70tr, c.20thC. Fox / Everett 19cl, 66, Erik C Pendzich 102cr, c.BuenaVist / Everett 62l, c.Focus / Everett 59r, c.MGM / Everett 61l, c.Universal / Everett 59tl, 59bl, Courtesy Everett Collection 70l, Everett Collection 59c, Mirta Lispi 102bc (Eminem), Quirky China News 19l, Brian Rasic 69l, 69c, 72b, SNAP 60l, United Artists / Everett 60r; **Science Photo Library Ltd:** Laguna Design 22b; **Shutterstock.com:** runzelkorn 29tl

**Cover images:** *Front:* **Pearson Education Ltd:** Gareth Boden t; **Photolibrary.com:** Blend Images RM / Hill Street Studios br, Britain on View / Howard Taylor tr, Juice Images bl, OJO Images / Paul Bradbury tl

All other images © Pearson Education

Every effort has been made to trace the copyright holders and we apologise in advance for any unintentional omissions. We would be pleased to insert the appropriate acknowledgement in any subsequent edition of this publication.